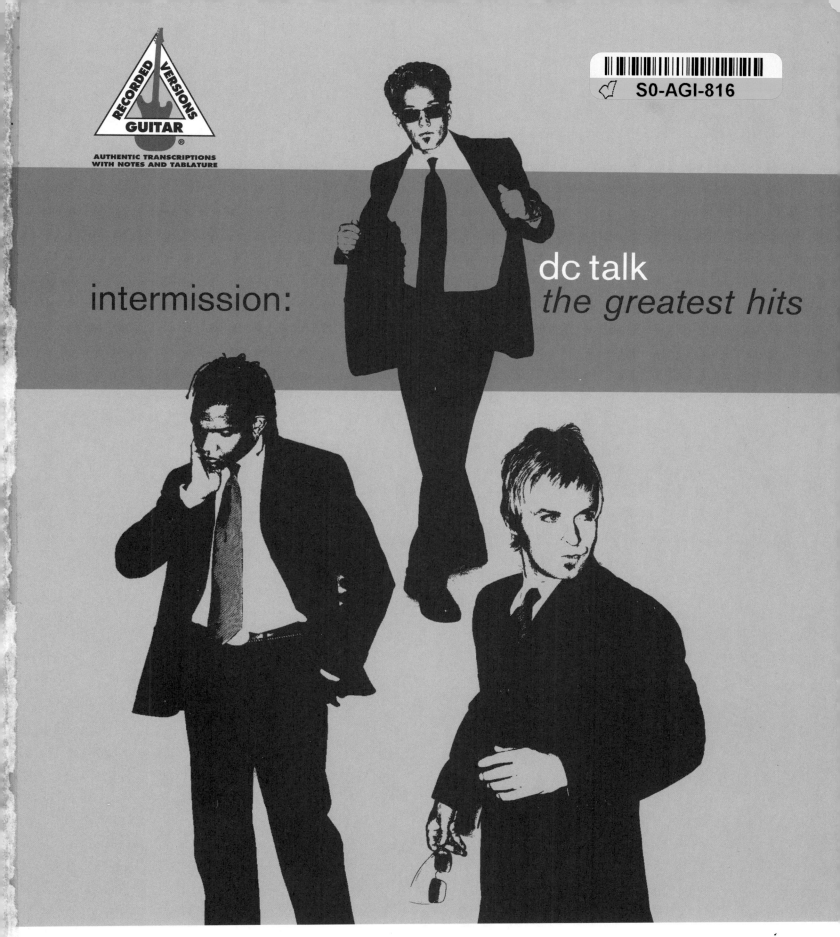

intermission: dc talk *the greatest hits*

RECORDED VERSIONS GUITAR ®

AUTHENTIC TRANSCRIPTIONS
WITH NOTES AND TABLATURE

S0-AGI-816

ISBN 0-634-02959-2

HAL•LEONARD®
CORPORATION

7777 W. BLUEMOUND RD. P.O. BOX 13819 MILWAUKEE, WI 53213

Visit Hal Leonard Online at
www.halleonard.com

contents

Say the Words

Words and Music by Toby McKeehan and Mark Heimermann

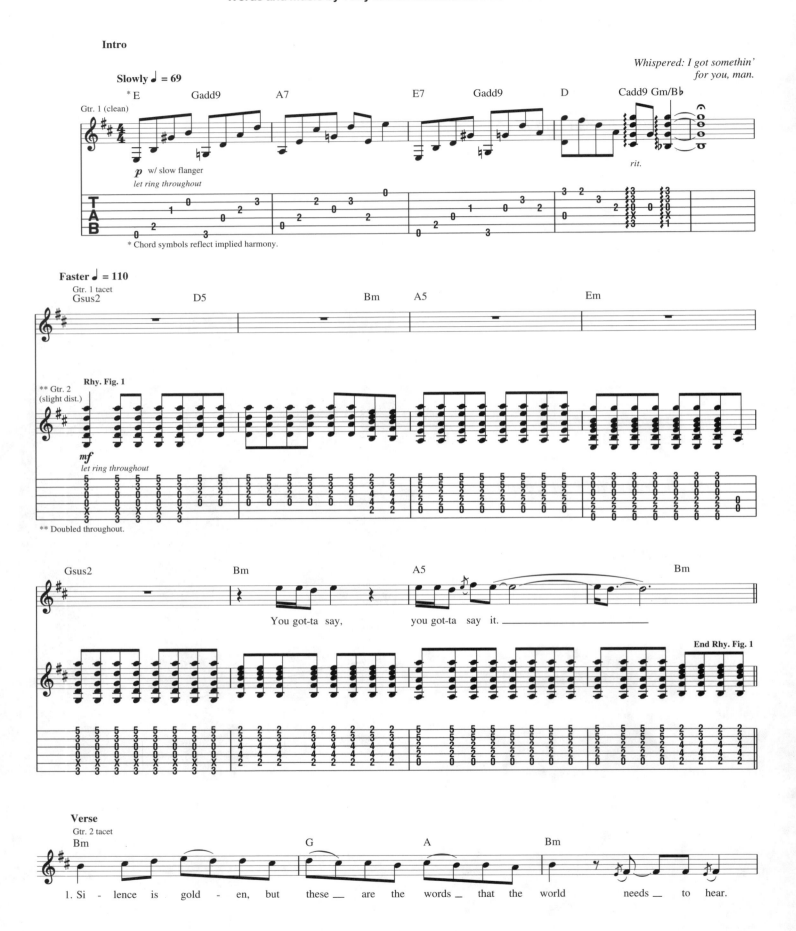

Chorus

Gtr. 2: w/ Rhy. Fig. 1 (2 times)
2nd time, Gtr. 5: w/ Fill 3 (4 times)
Gtr. 3 tacet

Say the words, — say the words. Say "I love _____ you." —

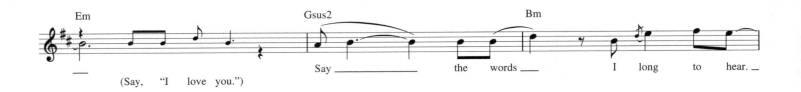

— (Say, "I love you.") Say _____ the words ___ I long to hear. —

_____ (I long to hear them.) _____ Oh, won't you say the words, — say

the words. Say "I love _____ you." ___ (Say, "I love you.") _____

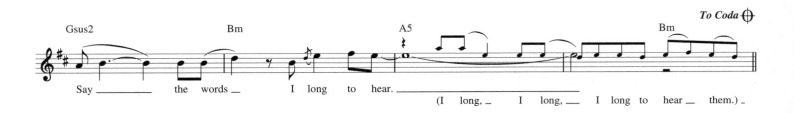

Say _____ the words — I long to hear. _____ (I long, — I long, — I long to hear — them.) _

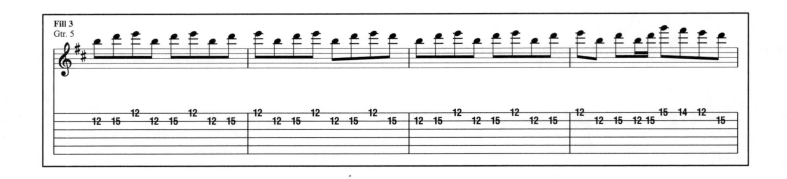

-fuse ___ to let love be di-lut-ed. We can't al-low phy-si-cal lust ___ to in-trude it

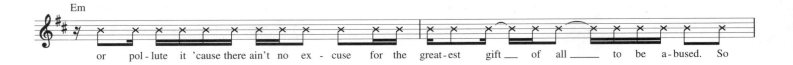

or pol-lute it 'cause there ain't no ex-cuse for the great-est gift ___ of all ___ to be a-bused. So

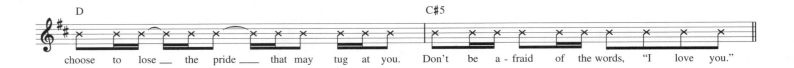

choose to lose ___ the pride ___ that may tug at you. Don't be a-fraid of the words, "I love you."

Chorus

Say the words, ___ say the words. Say, "I love ___ you." ___

Say ___ the words ___ I long to hear. ___ (I long to hear them.) ___

Gtr. 2: w/ Rhy. Fig. 1 (till fade)   Bkgd. Voc.: w/ Voc. Fig. 2

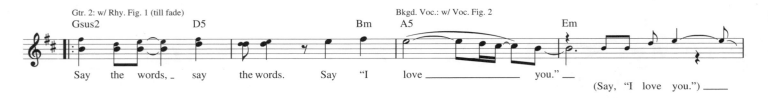

Say the words, ___ say the words. Say "I love ___ you." ___ (Say, "I love you.") ___

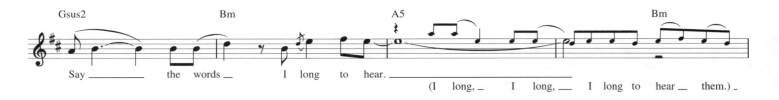

Say ___ the words ___ I long to hear. ___ (I long, ___ I long, ___ I long to hear ___ them.) ___

Bkgd. Voc.: w/ Voc. Fig. 1

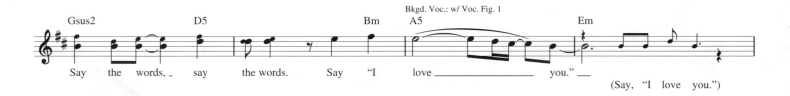

Say the words, ___ say the words. Say "I love ___ you." (Say, "I love you.")

Repeat & fade

Say ___ the words ___ I long to hear. ___ Oh, won't you (I long to hear them.) ___

Colored People

Words and Music by Toby McKeehan and George Cocchini

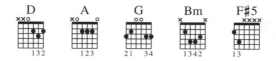

* Chord symbols reflect implied tonality.

(One, one, one, one, two, two, two, two, three, three, three, three, four, four, four, four.)

** echo repeats

Interlude

Chorus

13

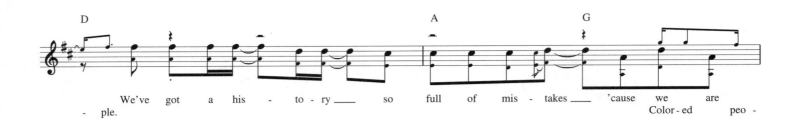

We've got a his - to - ry ___ so full of mis - takes ___ 'cause we are

- ple. Color - ed peo -

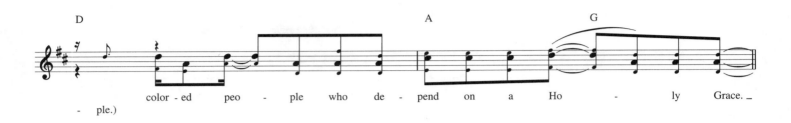

- ple.) col - or - ed peo - ple who de - pend on a Ho - ly Grace. ___

Outro-Chorus
Gtrs. 1, 2 & 3: w/ Rhy. Figs. 1, 1A & 1B, 5 times, simile

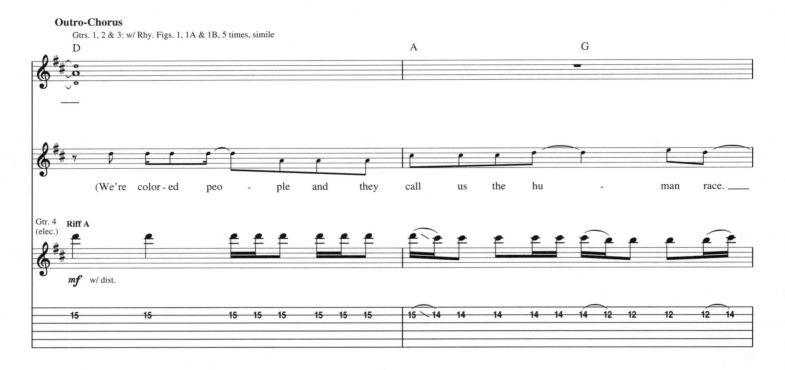

(We're col - or - ed peo - ple and they call us the hu - man race. ___

Gtr. 4
(elec.)
Riff A

mf w/ dist.

```
15        15         15  15  15   15  15  15   15  14  14   14   14  14  14  12  12   12   12  14
```

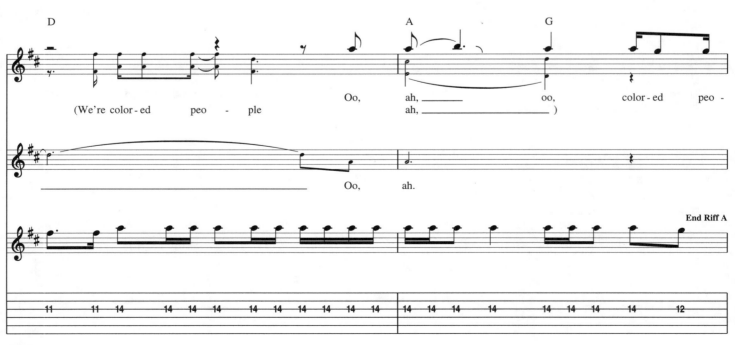

(We're col - or - ed peo - ple

Oo, ah, ___ oo, col - or - ed peo -

ah, ___)

Oo, ah.

End Riff A

```
11    11  14      14  14  14   14  14  14  14   14  14  14   14      14  14  14   14        12
```

Additional Lyrics

2. A piece of canvas is only the beginning,
   For it takes on character with every loving stroke.
   This thing of beauty is the passion of an artist's heart.
   By God's design, we are a skin kaleidoscope.

Pre-Chorus: We gotta come together,
            Aren't we human after all?

Jesus Is Just Alright

Words and Music by Arthur Reynolds

Chorus

Gtr. 1: w/ Rhy. Fig. 1 (3 1/2 times)

Je - sus is still al - right ____ with me. ____ Je - sus is still al - right, ____

Gtr. 4 (dist.)

mf

H.H. - - - - - - - - -

* Harmonic & fretted note sound simultaneously.

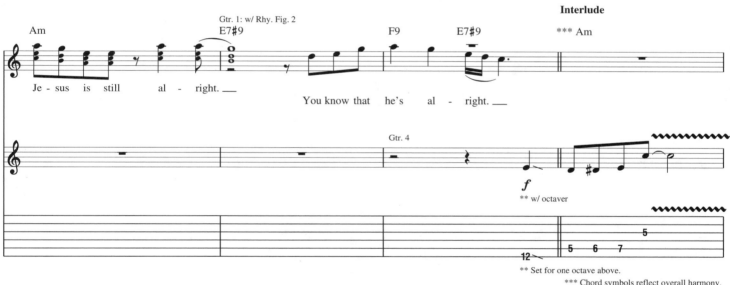

Gtr. 4 tacet

____ oh yeah. ____ Je - sus is still al - right ____ with me. ____

Interlude

Gtr. 1: w/ Rhy. Fig. 2

Je - sus is still al - right. ____ You know that he's al - right. ____

Gtr. 4

f

** w/ octaver

** Set for one octave above.

*** Chord symbols reflect overall harmony.

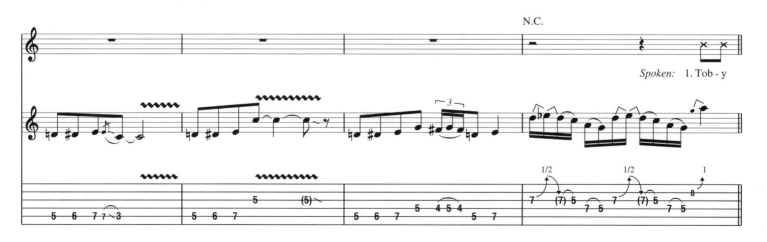

N.C.

Spoken: 1. Tob - y

Verse

Chorus

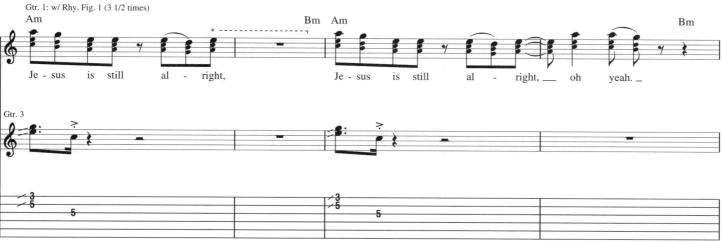

* w/ Echo set for quarter note regeneration w/ 3 repeats.

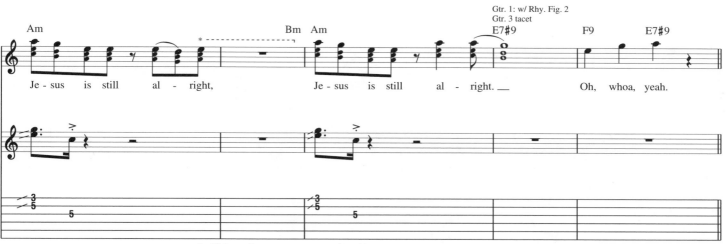

* w/ Echo set for quarter note regeneration w/ 3 repeats.

Interlude

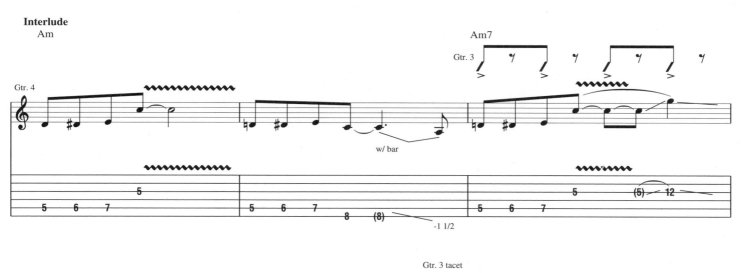

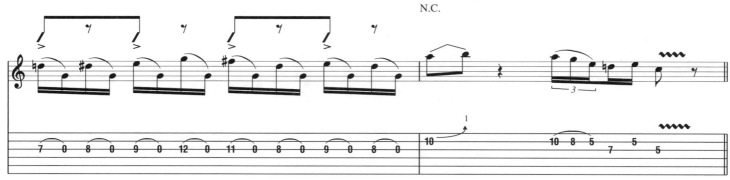

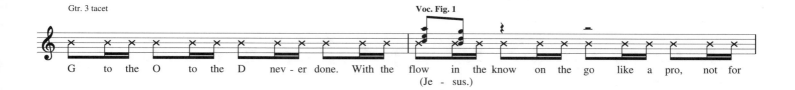

G to the O to the D nev-er done. With the flow in the know on the go like a pro, not for
(Je - sus.)

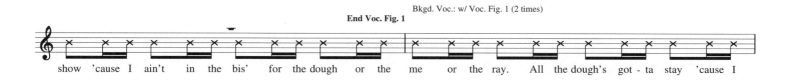

Bkgd. Voc.: w/ Voc. Fig. 1 (2 times)
End Voc. Fig. 1

show 'cause I ain't in the bis' for the dough or the me or the ray. All the dough's got-ta stay 'cause I

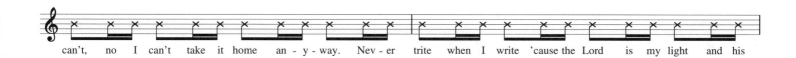

can't, no I can't take it home an-y-way. Nev-er trite when I write 'cause the Lord is my light and his

Chorus
Gtr. 1: w/ Rhy. Fig. 1 (3 1/2 times)
Gtr. 4: w/ Riff A

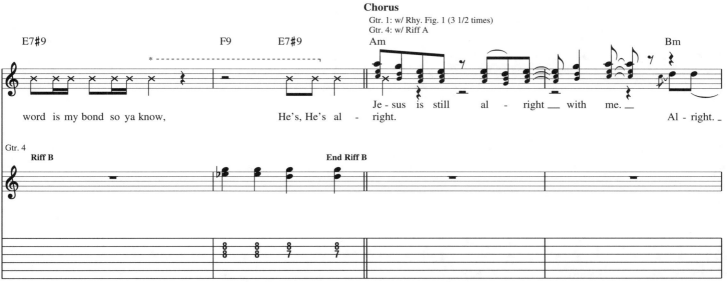

word is my bond so ya know,   He's, He's al - right.   Al - right.

Je - sus is still al - right ___ with me.

Gtr. 4
Riff B   End Riff B

* w/ Echo, set for quarter note regeneration, gradually decreasing delay time to eighth note regeneration.

Je - sus is still al - right,___ oh yeah. ___   Je - sus is still al - right ___
                                        Oh yeah.

Gtr. 1: w/ Rhy. Fig. 2
Gtr. 4: w/ Riff B

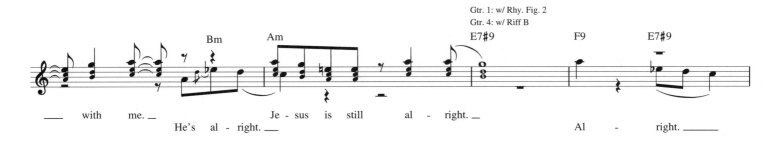

___ with me. ___   Je - sus is still al - right. ___   Al -   right. _____
        He's al - right. ___

Between You and Me

Words and Music by Toby McKeehan and Mark Heimermann

Pre-Chorus

If there's to be an-y res - o - lu - tion, _____
We've got a love that's _____ worth pre - serv - in', _____

I've got to peel my pride _____ a - way. _____
and a bond I will de - fend. _____

Chorus

Gtrs. 3, 4 & 5 tacet

Just be-tween you and me, I've got some-thin' to say, wan-na get it straight

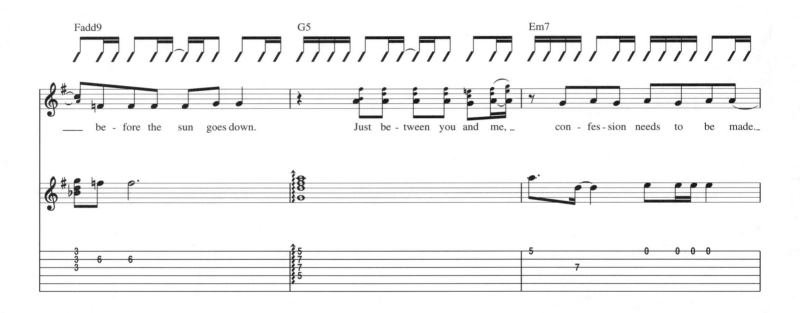

be-fore the sun goes down. Just be-tween you and me, con-fes-sion needs to be made.

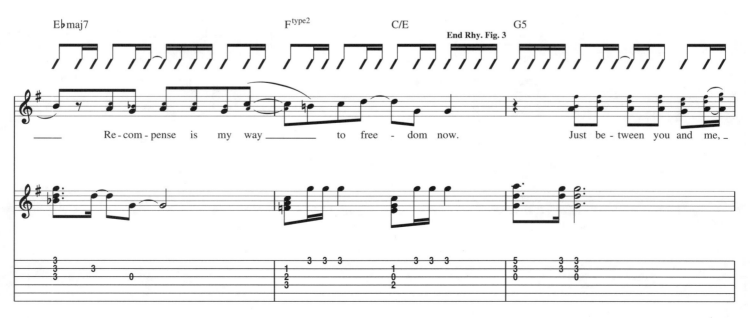

Re-com-pense is my way to free-dom now. Just be-tween you and me,

I've got some-thing to say. _____ Say. (echo repeats) 2. If con -

Bridge
A Tempo

In my pur - suit of God, I thirst for ho - li - ness. As I ap - proach the Son,

Gtr. 8

* vol. swell

Gtr. 7

delay off
slight P.M. throughout

I must con - sid - er this. Of - fen - ces un - re - solved will keep me from the throne.

Be - fore I go to Him, my wrong must be a -

Pre-Chorus

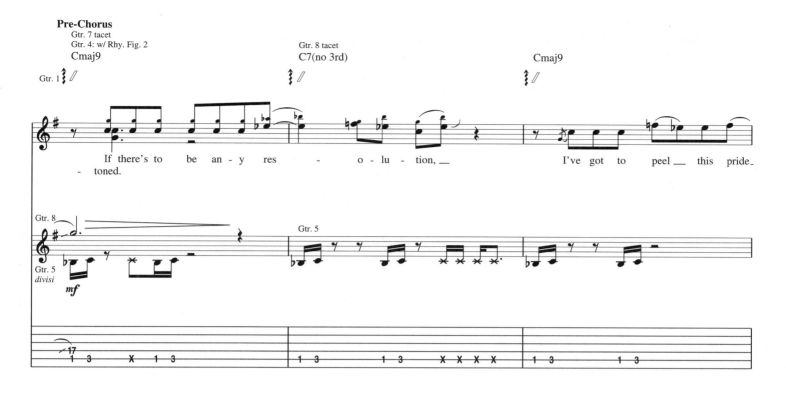

If there's to be an-y res - o-lu - tion, __ I've got to peel __ this pride __
- toned.

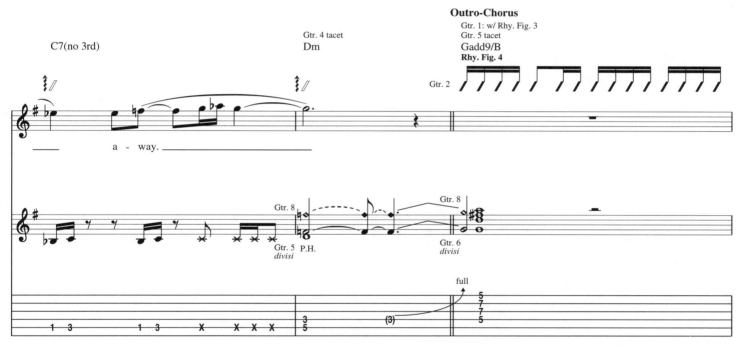

a - way. __

Outro-Chorus

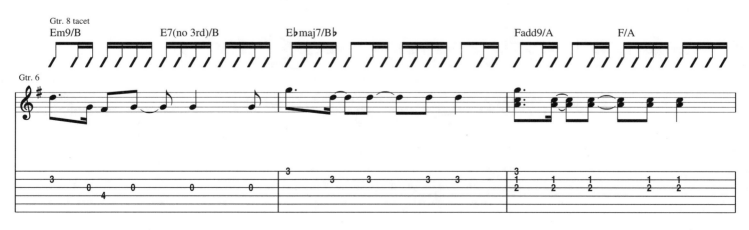

Mind's Eye

Words and Music by Toby McKeehan, Michael Tait and Mark Heimermann

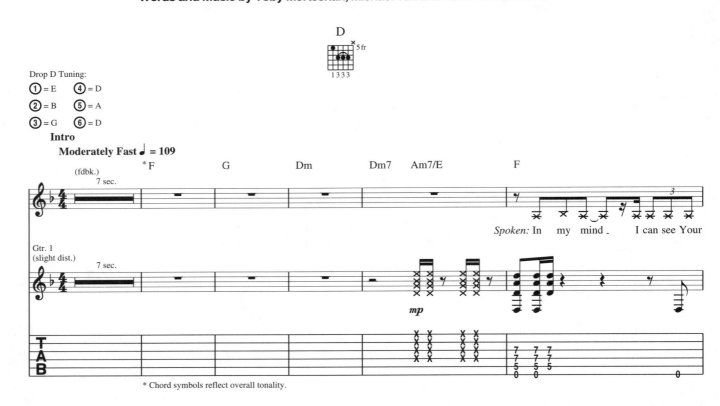

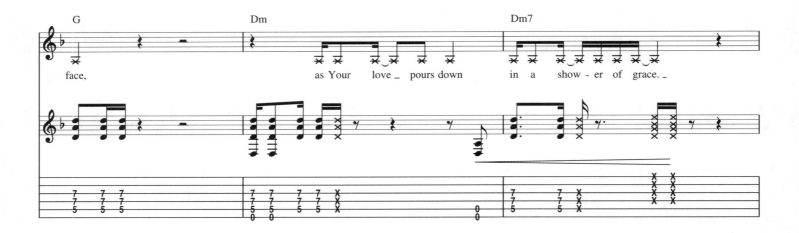

as You show me grace. In my mind's eye You

In my mind.

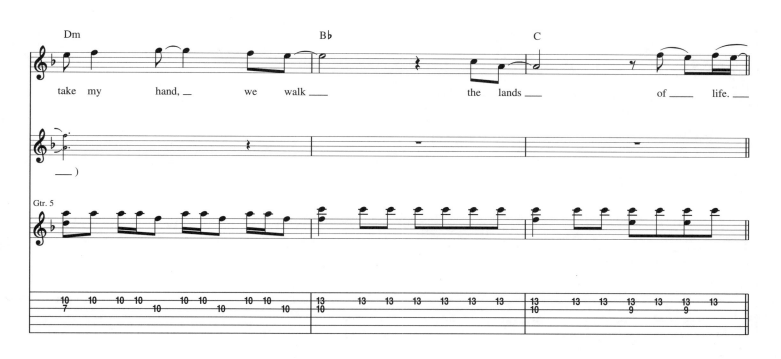

take my hand, we walk the lands of life.
_)

Gtr. 5

Interlude

Bkgd. Voc.: w/ Voc. Fig. 1
Gtr. 5 tacet

D   C/D   G   Gsus4

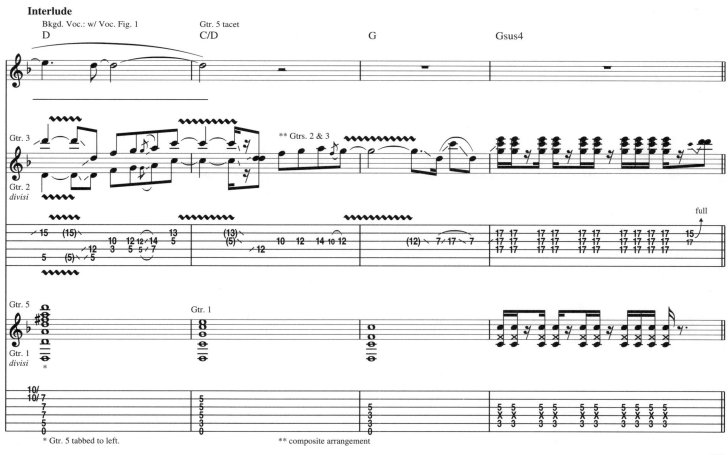

Gtr. 3

** Gtrs. 2 & 3

full

Gtr. 2
divisi

Gtr. 5

Gtr. 1

Gtr. 1
divisi

*

* Gtr. 5 tabbed to left.   ** composite arrangement

Outro-Chorus

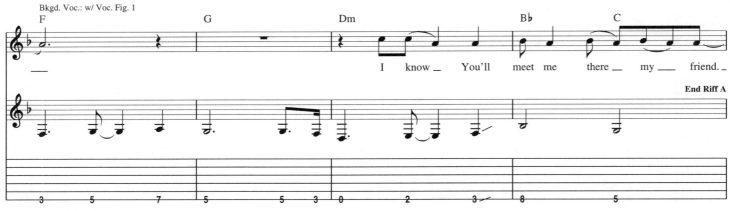

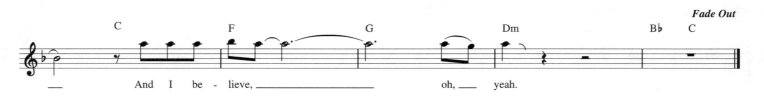

42

Consume Me

Words and Music by Toby McKeehan, Michael Tait, Kevin Max and Mark Heimermann

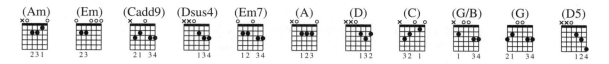

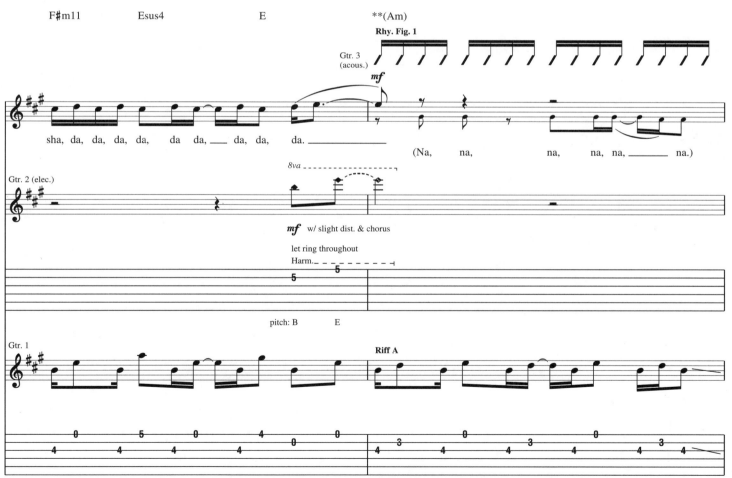

Sha, da, da, da, da, da, da. _____

(Na, na, na, na, na, _____ na.)

Verse

Gtrs. 1, 2, & 3 tacet

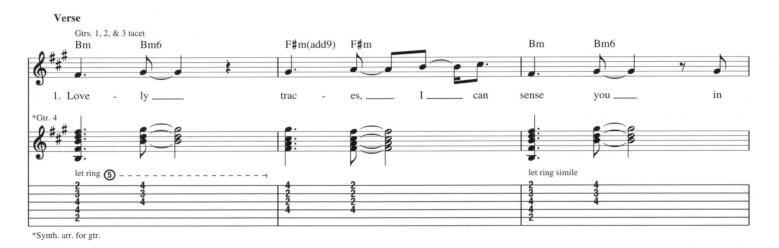

1. Love - ly _____ trac - es, _____ I _____ can sense you _____ in

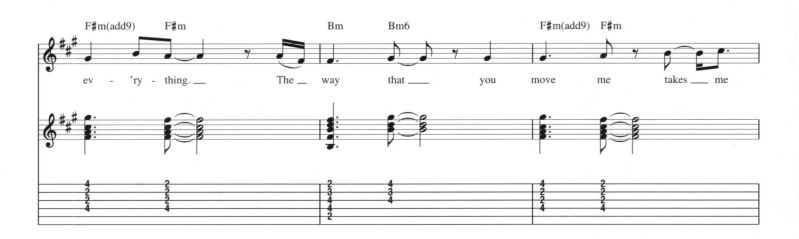

ev - 'ry - thing. _____ The _____ way that _____ you move me takes _____ me

*Synth. arr. for gtr.

*Increase depth setting on chorus to simulate vibrato effect.

Verse

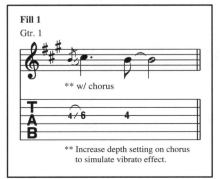

Pre-Chorus

way that you de-liv-er me. ___ (I'm ___ tran - scend - ed. ___) There's no place I'd rath - er be... ___ ...than

(I'm tran - scend - ed. ___

here ___ in heav - en. ___) With-out you I'm in-com-plete. ___ It's hope - less. You con-sume ___

Here in heav - en. ___)

Chorus

*Symbols in parentheses represent chord names respective to capoed guitar. Symbols above reflect actual sounding chord. Capoed fret is "0" in TAB.

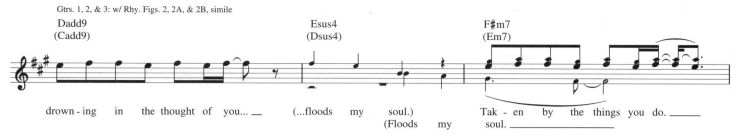

drown-ing in the thought of you... _____ (...floods my soul.) Tak-en by the things you do. _____
(Floods my soul. _____)

(God, you know it...) ...does-n't mat-ter what I lose. _ I'm yours. _____ You con-sume _
God, you know. _____)

Chorus

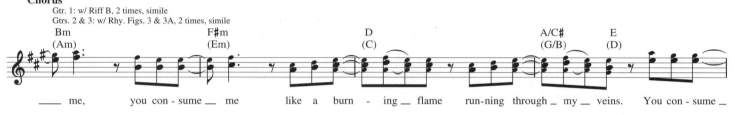

_____ me, you con-sume _ me like a burn-ing _ flame run-ning through _ my _ veins. You con-sume _

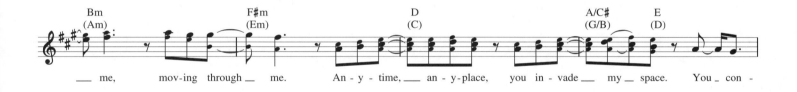

_____ me, mov-ing through _ me. An-y-time, _____ an-y-place, you in-vade _ my _ space. You con-

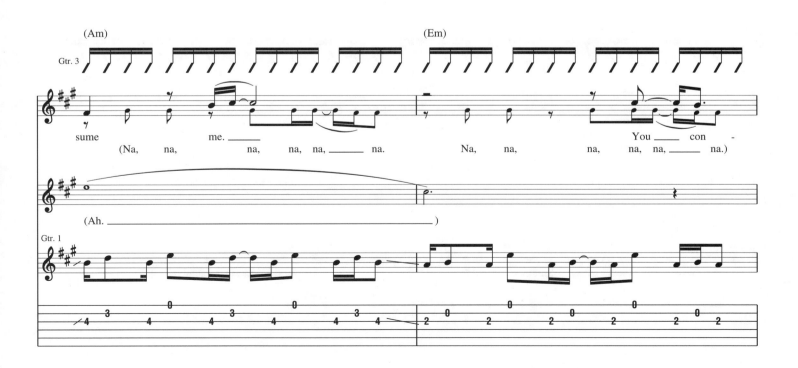

sume me. _____
(Na, na, na, na, na, _____ na. Na, na, na, na, na, _____ na.)

(Ah. _____)

Gtr. 1

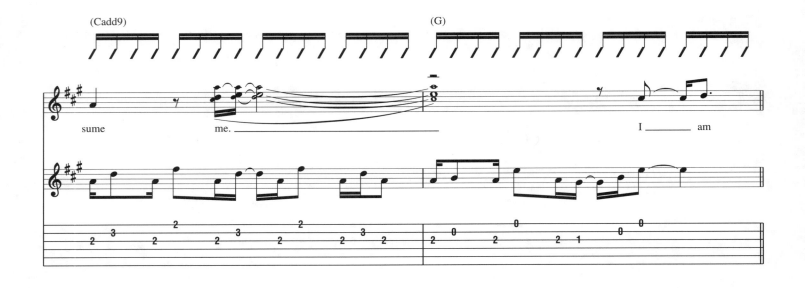

sume   me. _____   I _____ am

Bridge

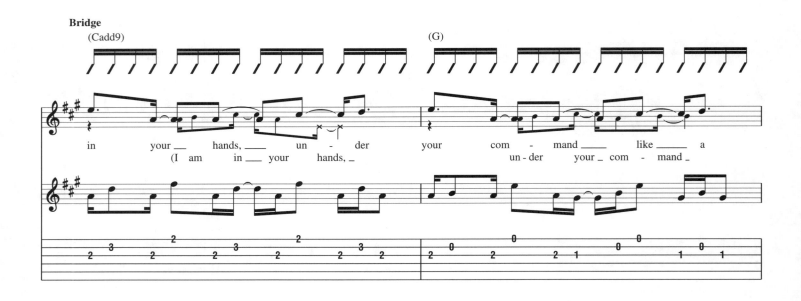

in   your ___ hands, ____   un - der   your   com - mand _____   like _____ a
(I   am   in ___ your   hands, _   un - der   your _ com - mand _

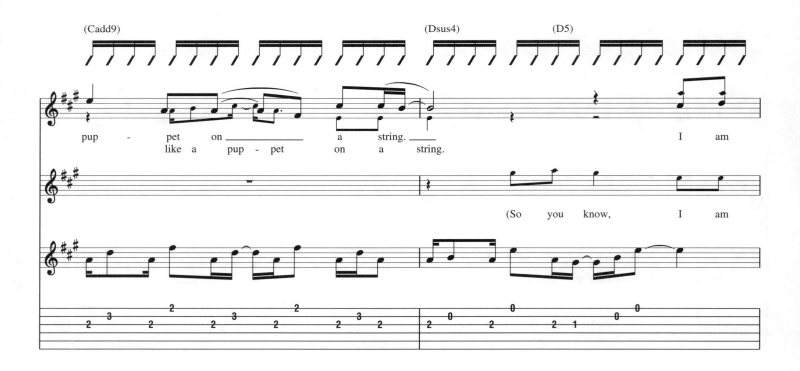

pup - pet   on _____   a   string. _____   I   am
like a   pup - pet   on   a   string.

(So   you   know,   I   am

Interlude

Gtr. 1: w/ Riff B, 2 times, simile
Gtrs. 2 & 3 tacet

Outro

Gtr. 1: w/ Riff B, 4 times, simile
*Gtr. 2: w/ Rhy. Fig. 3, 2 times, simile
Gtr. 3: w/ Rhy. Fig. 3A, simile, till fade

*flanger off

Gtr. 5: w/ Rhy. Fig. 4, simile, till fade

My Will

Words and Music by Toby McKeehan, Michael Tait, Joey Elwood and Daniel Pitts

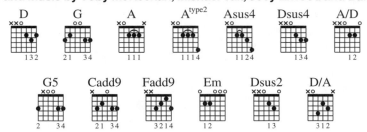

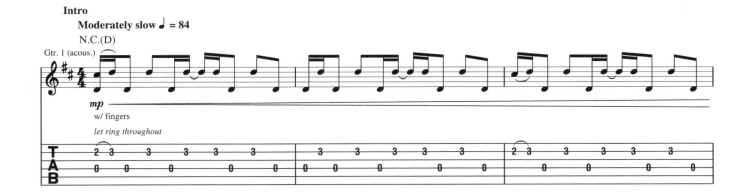

*Chord symbols reflect implied harmony.

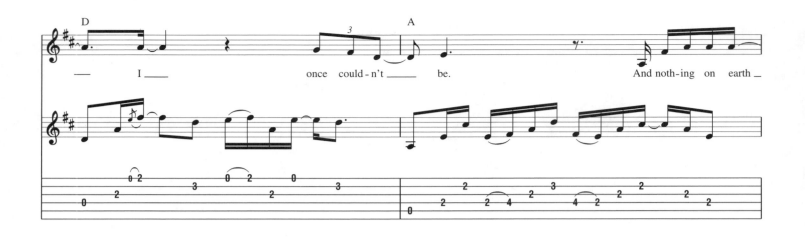

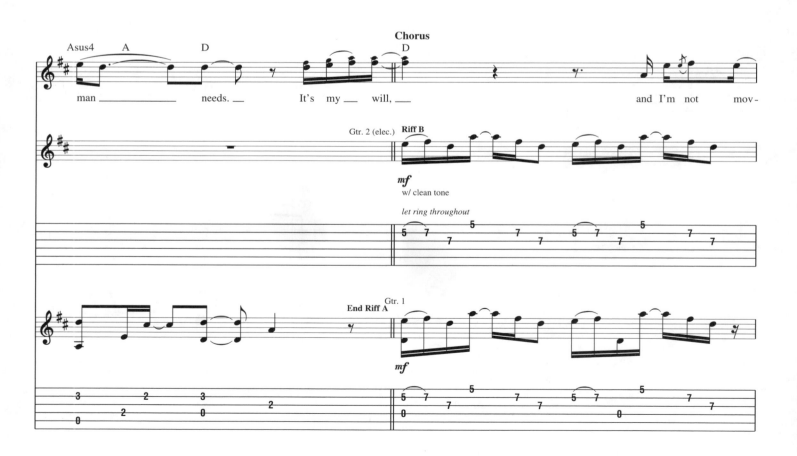

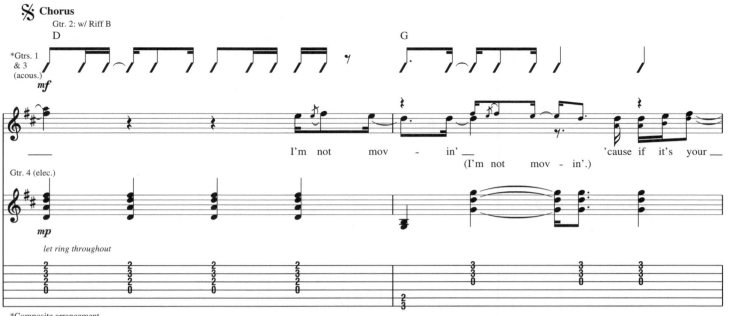

*Composite arrangement.

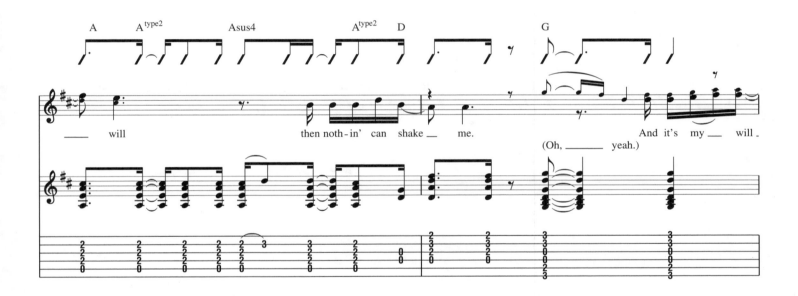

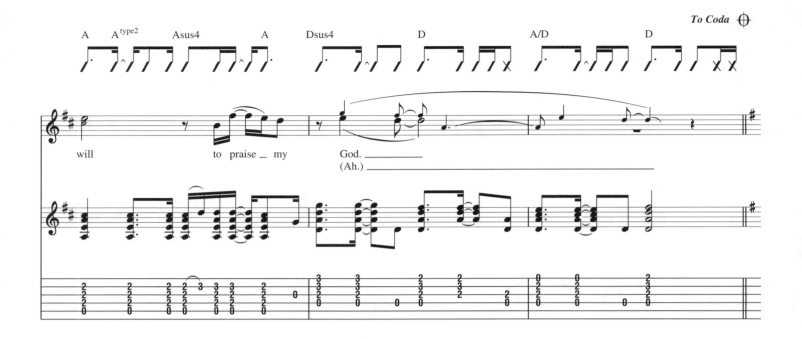

Interlude

3. I'm learn-in' to give

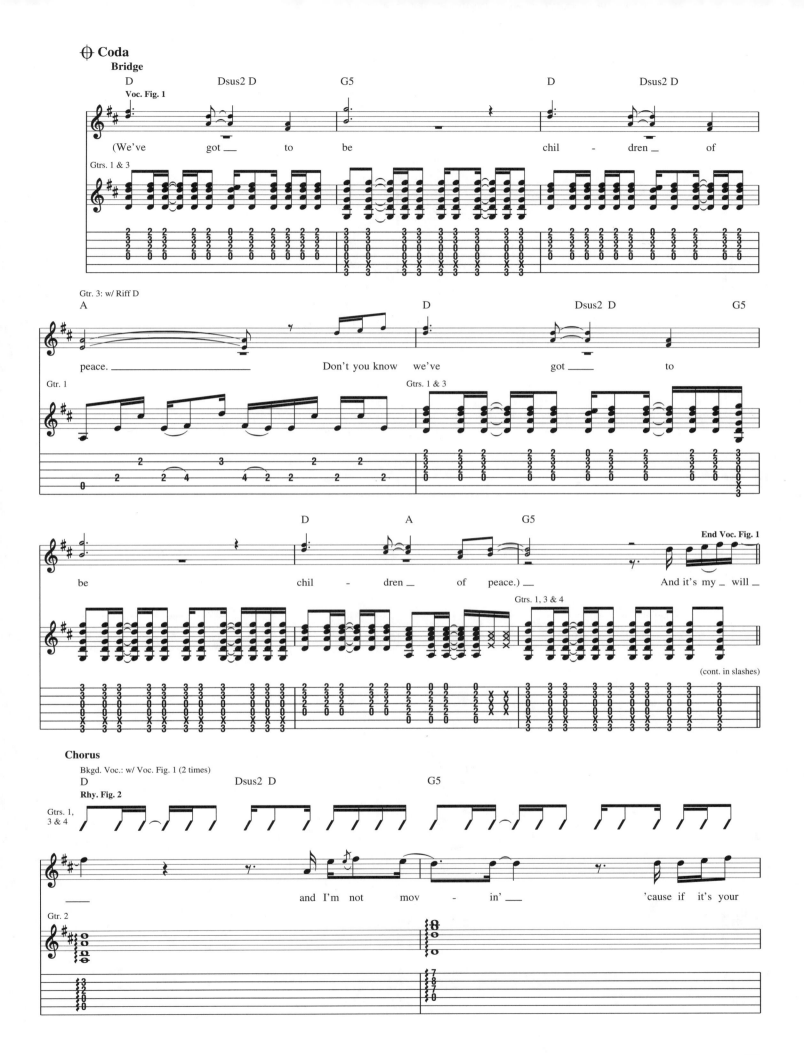

will   then noth-ing can shake _ me. _____   And it's my _ will _

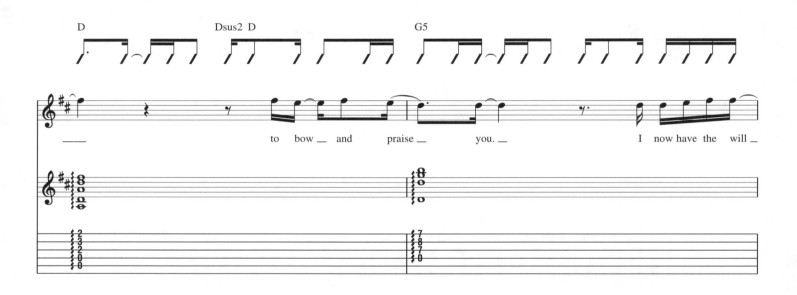

_   to bow _ and   praise _   you. _   I now have the   will _

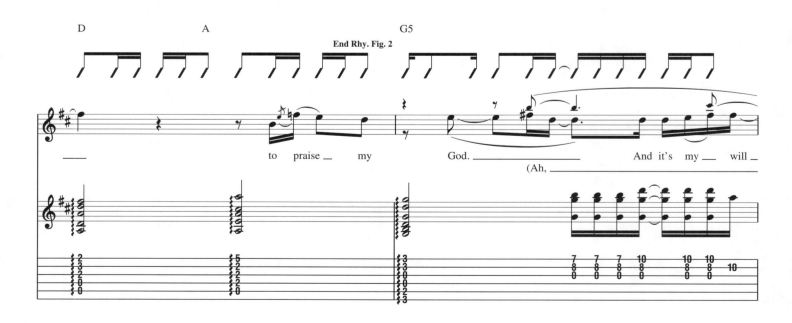

_   to praise _   my   God. _____   And it's my _ will _

(Ah, _____

Interlude

Gtrs. 1 & 3: w/ Rhy. Fig. 1 (2 times)
Gtr. 2: w/ Riff C (1 3/4 times)

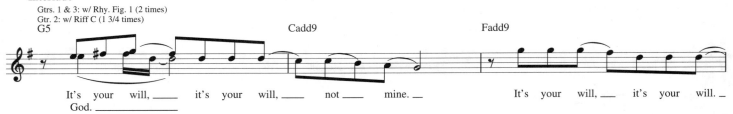

It's your will, _____ it's your will, _____ not _____ mine. _____
God. _____

It's your will, _____ it's your will, _____ not _____ mine. _____

Outro Chorus

Bkgd. Voc.: w/ Voc. Fig. 1 (1st 7 meas.)

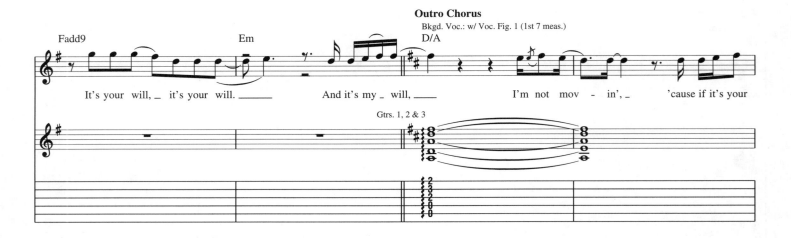

It's your will, _ it's your will. _____   And it's my _ will, _____   I'm not mov - in', _   'cause if it's your

Gtrs. 1, 2 & 3

Gtrs. 1, 2 & 3 tacet

will   then noth-ing can save _ me. _____   And it's my _ will _   to bow _ and praise _

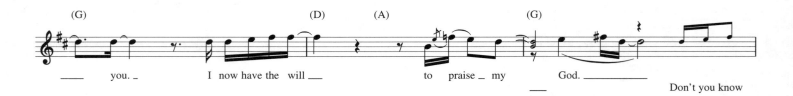

_____ you. _   I now have the will _   to praise _ my   God. _____
Don't you know

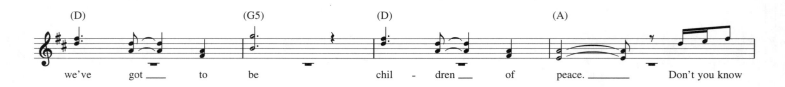

we've   got _____ to   be   chil - dren _____ of   peace. _____   Don't you know

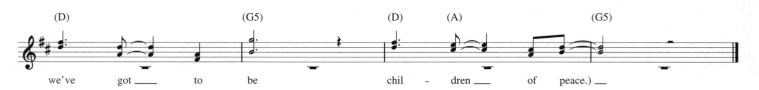

we've   got _____ to   be   chil - dren _____ of   peace.) _____

In the Light

Words and Music by Charlie Peacock

Pre-Chorus

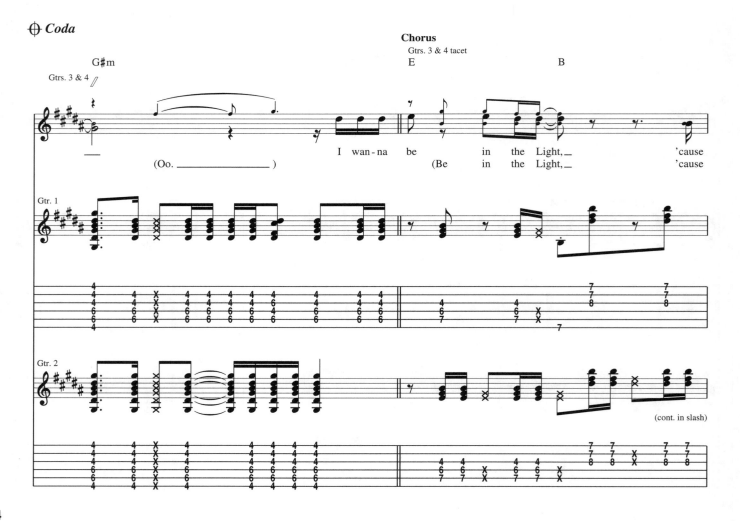

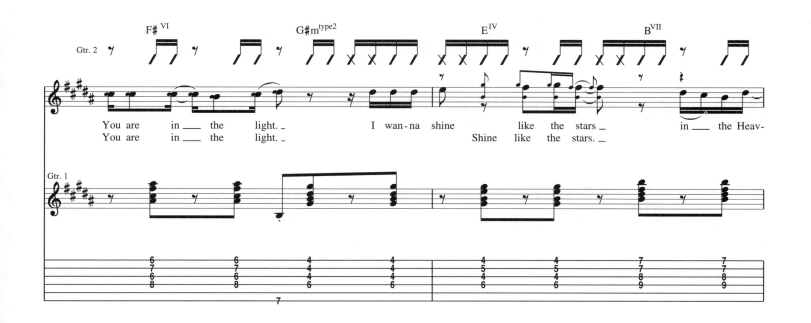

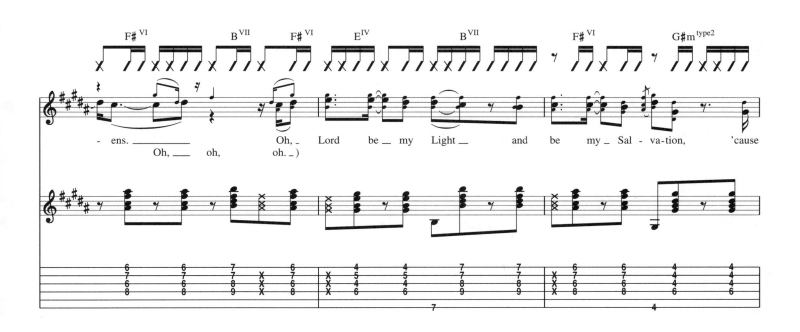

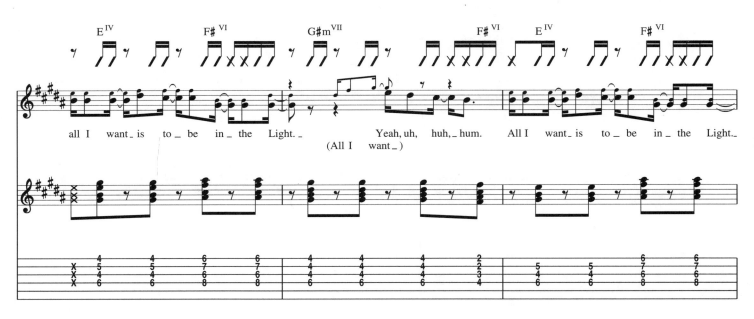

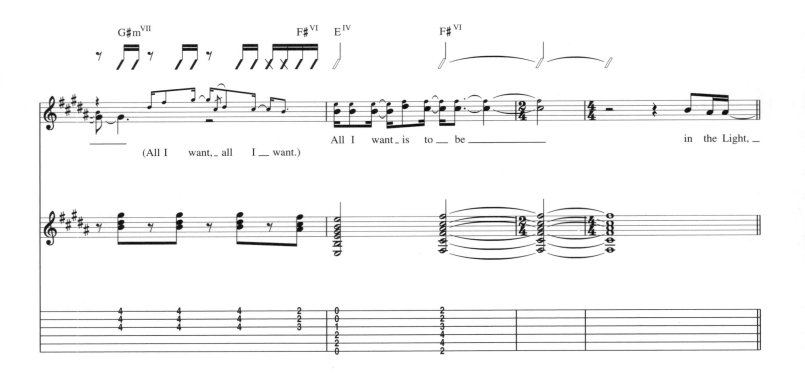

Outro-Chorus

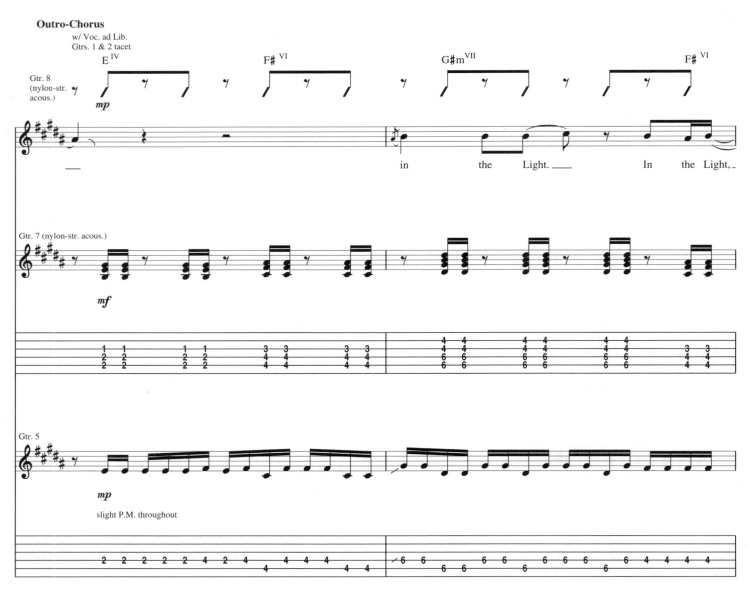

Socially Acceptable

Words and Music by Toby McKeehan and Mark Heimermann

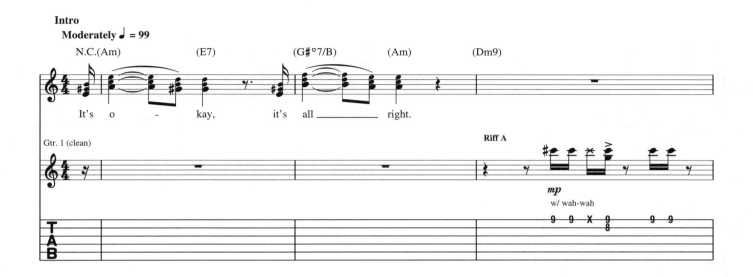

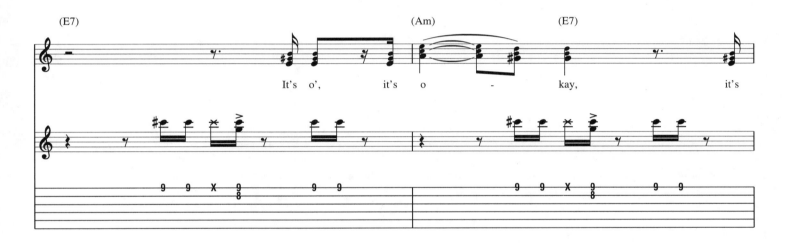

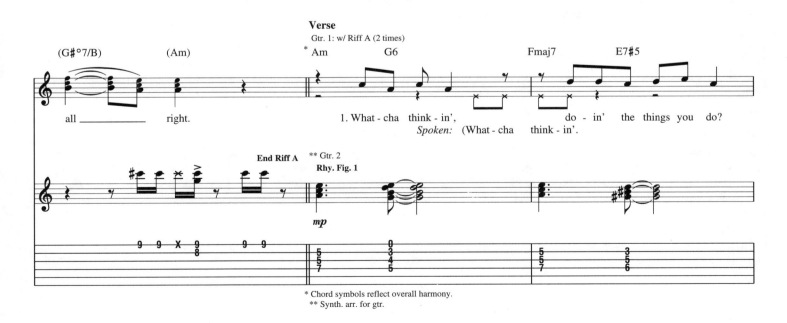

* Chord symbols reflect overall harmony.
** Synth. arr. for gtr.

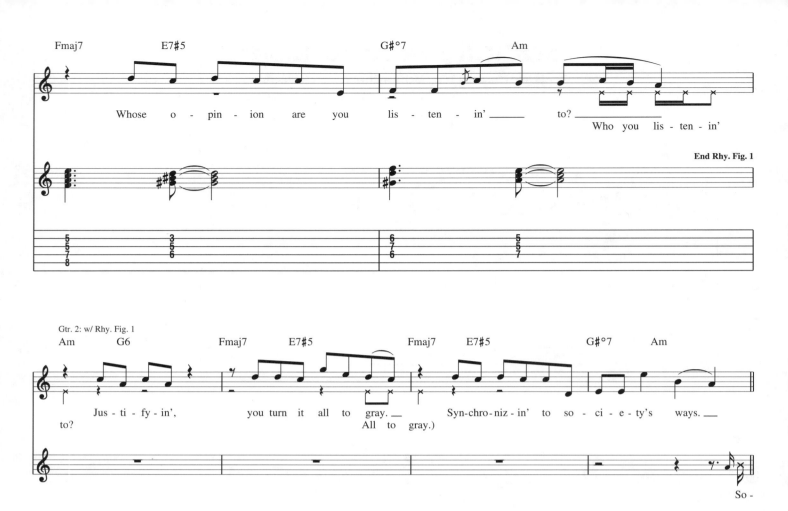

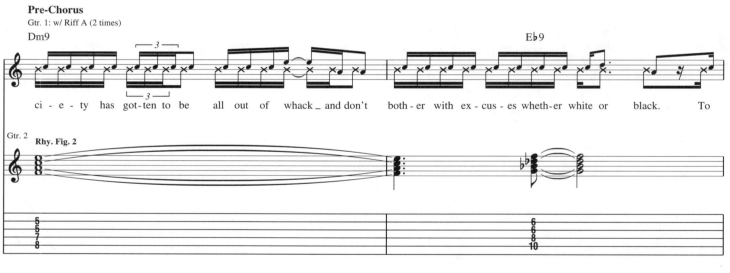

Pre-Chorus

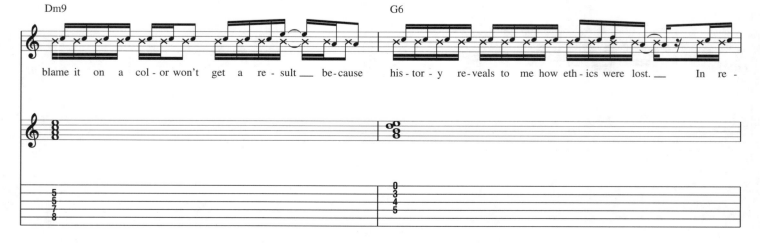

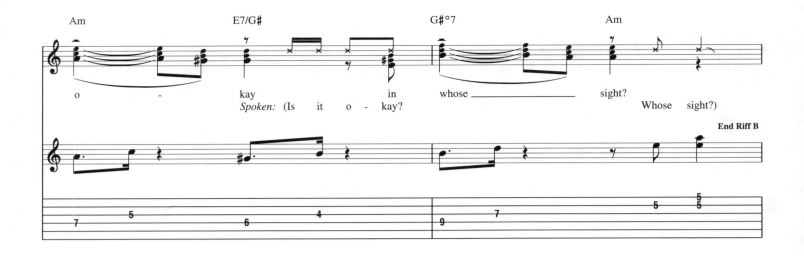

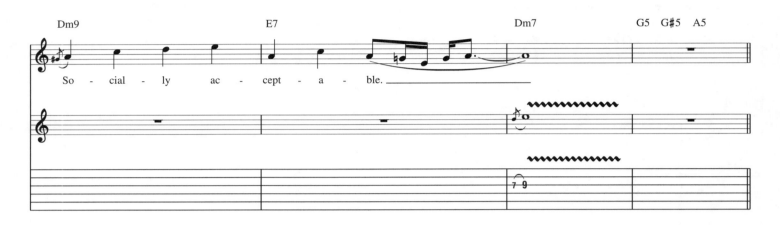

Verse

Gtr. 1: w/ Riff A (2 times)
Gtr. 2: w/ Rhy. Fig. 1 (2 times)

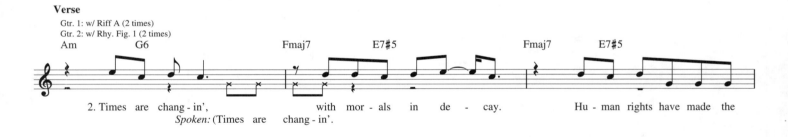

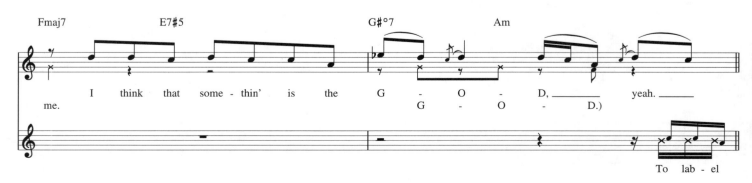

Pre-Chorus

Gtr. 1: w/ Riff A (2 times)
Gtr. 2: w/ Rhy. Fig. 2

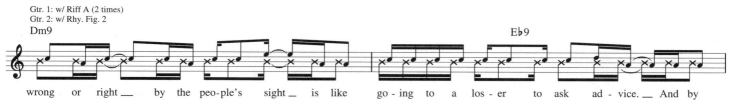

wrong or right __ by the peo-ple's sight __ is like go-ing to a los-er to ask ad-vice. __ And by

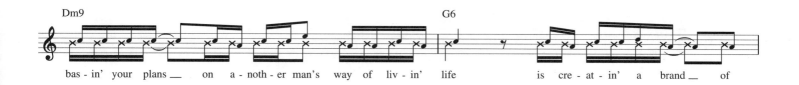

bas-in' your plans __ on a-noth-er man's way of liv-in' life is cre-at-in' a brand __ of

eth-ics sure to be miss-in' the punch, __ no count mor-als that are out to lunch. __ They're

slid-in' a-way __ 'cause ev-'ry-thing is o-kay. It was ta-boo back then, but to-day you say, __ "What the

Chorus

Gtr. 1: w/ Riff A (4 times)
Gtr. 3: w/ Riff B

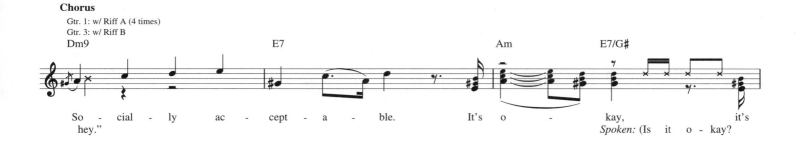

So - cial - ly ac-cept - a - ble. It's o - kay, it's
hey."
Spoken: (Is it o - kay?

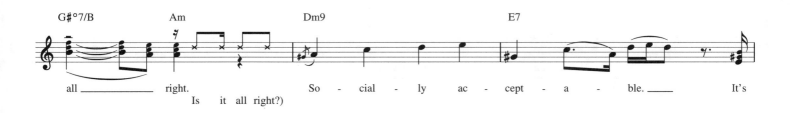

all _____ right. So - cial - ly ac-cept - a - ble. ___ It's
Is it all right?)

o - kay in whose _____ sight?
Spoken: (Is it o - kay? Whose sight?

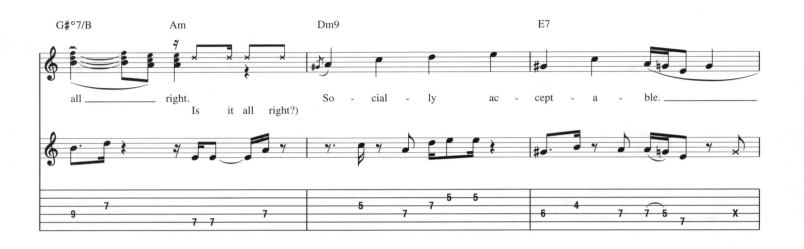

Interlude

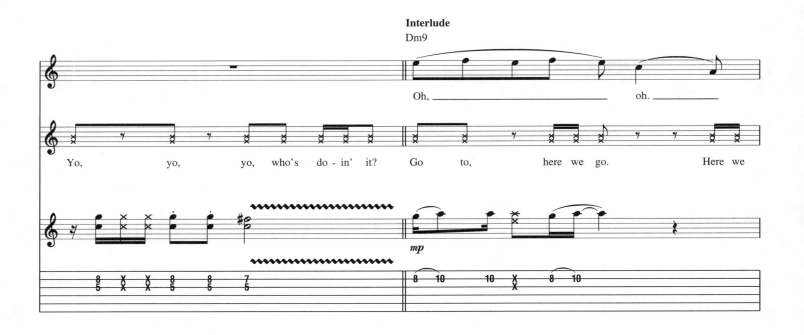

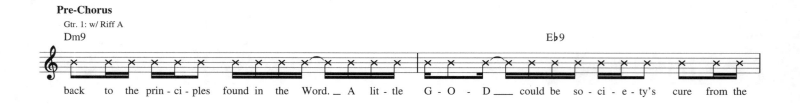

Pre-Chorus

Gtr. 1: w/ Riff A

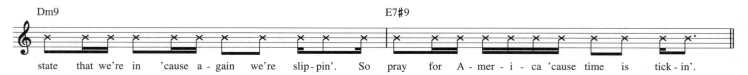

Chorus

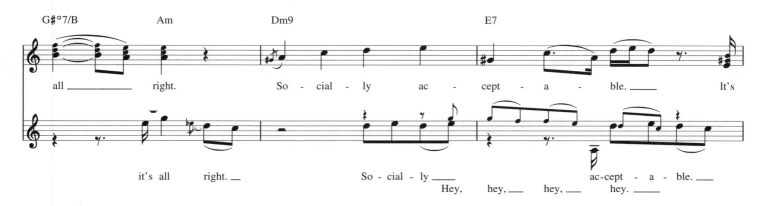

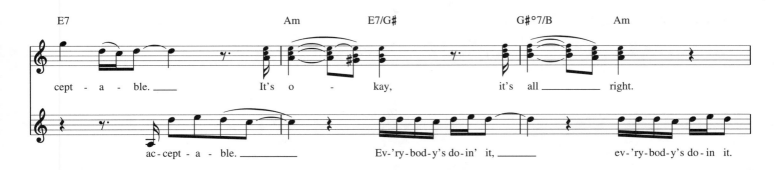

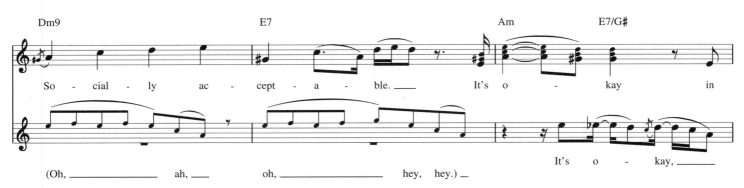

Outro

Gtr. 1: w/ Riff A (till end)

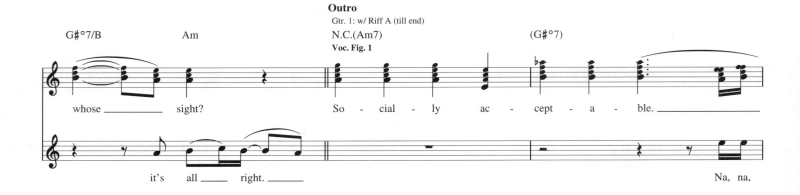

whose _____ sight? So - cial - ly ac - cept - a - ble. _____

it's all _____ right. _____ Na, na,

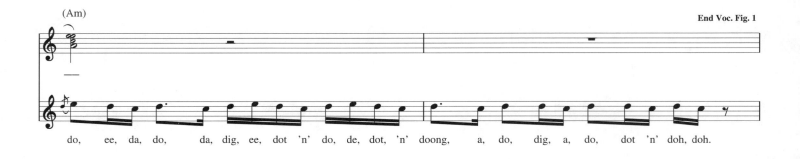

do, ee, da, do, da, dig, ee, dot 'n' do, de, dot, 'n' doong, a, do, dig, a, do, dot 'n' doh, doh.

Lead Voc.: w/ Voc. Fig. 1

Ze, ze, ba, de, da, de, da, da, do, de, dop. De,

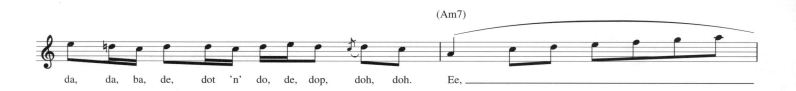

da, da, ba, de, dot 'n' do, de, dop, doh, doh. Ee, _____

Begin Fade

_____ hoo, _____ yeah, _ yeah, _____ yeah, yeah, _____ yeah, _ yeah, _____

Fade out

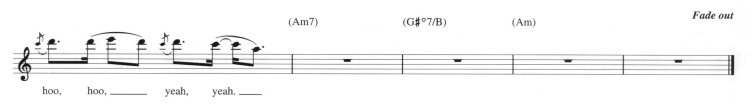

hoo, hoo, _____ yeah, yeah.

88

Luv Is a Verb

Words and Music by Toby McKeehan, Mark Heimermann and George Cocchini

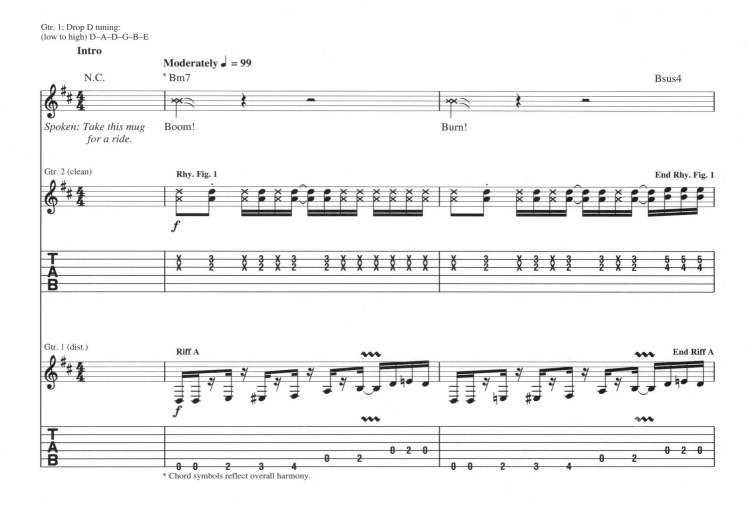

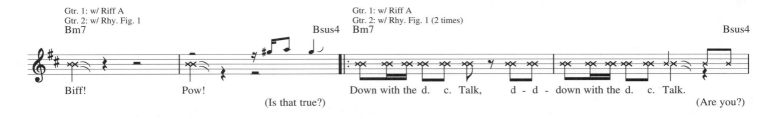

talk-in' 'bout love in a dif-f'rent light and if we all learn to love it will be ___ just right. ___

Chorus

Gtrs. 1 & 2 tacet
3rd time, Gtr. 6: w/ Fill 1 (2 times)

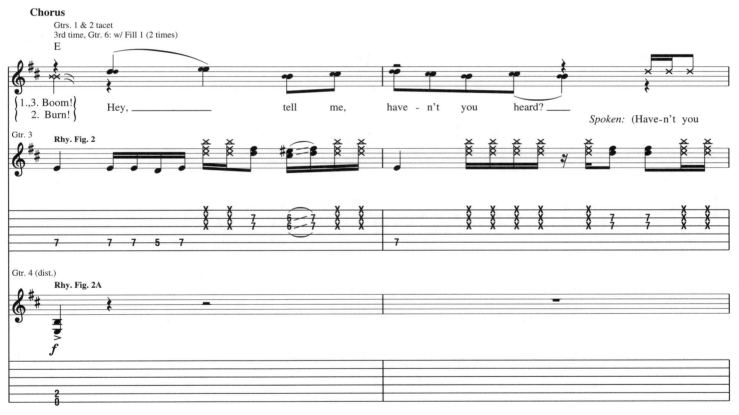

{1.,3. Boom!}
{2. Burn!}

Hey, _____ tell me, have-n't you heard? ___

Spoken: (Have-n't you

Gtr. 3 Rhy. Fig. 2

Gtr. 4 (dist.) Rhy. Fig. 2A

Fill 1
Gtr. 6 (clean)

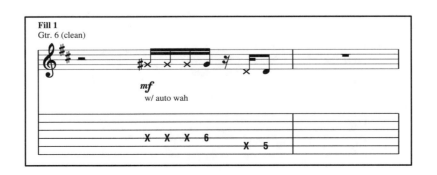

mf
w/ auto wah

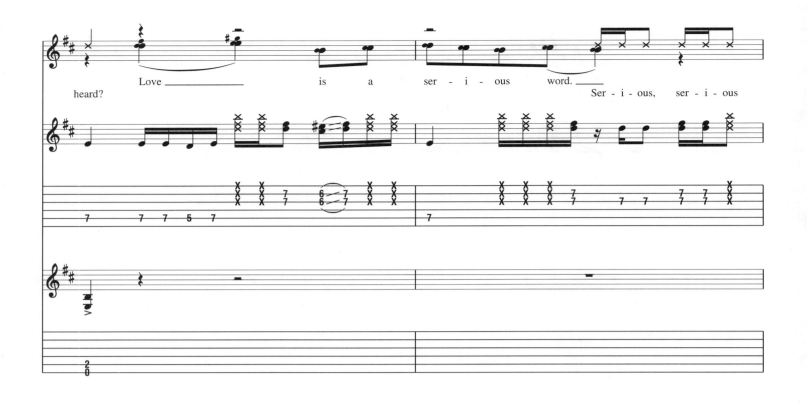

Love _____ is a ser - i - ous word. ____ Ser - i - ous, ser - i - ous

heard?

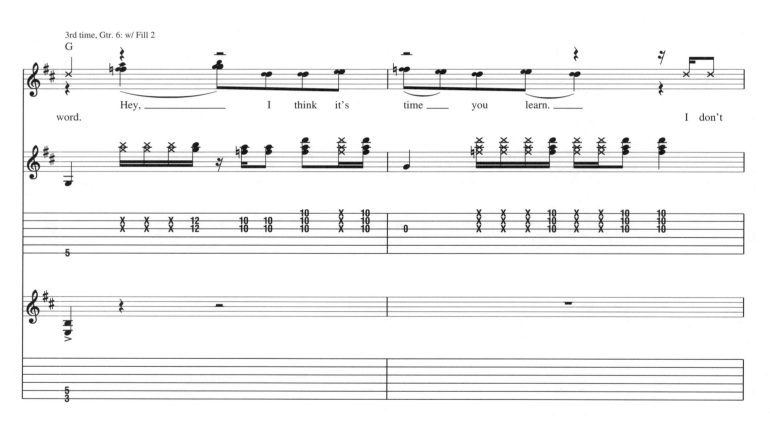

3rd time, Gtr. 6: w/ Fill 2

Hey, _____ I think it's time ____ you learn. ____ I don't

word.

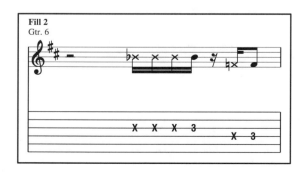

Fill 2
Gtr. 6

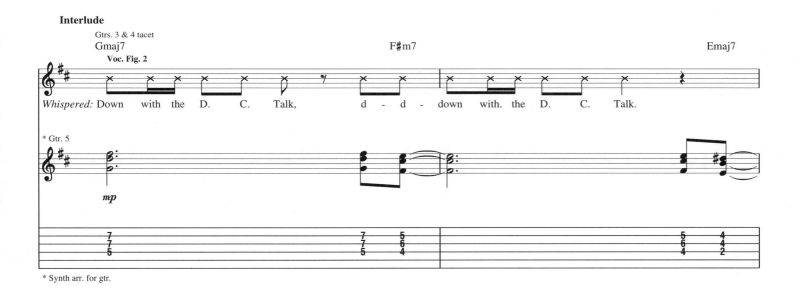

F#m7   Gmaj7

End Voc. Fig. 2

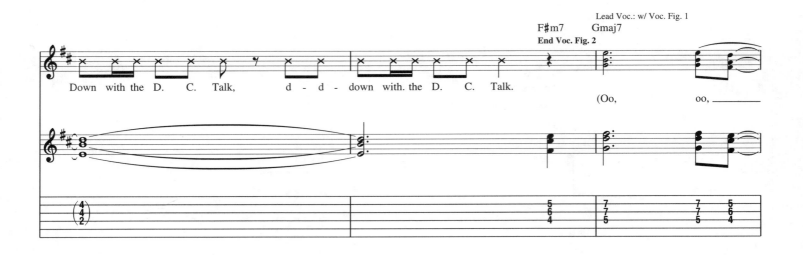

Down with the D. C. Talk,   d - d - down with. the D. C. Talk.   (Oo,   oo, _____

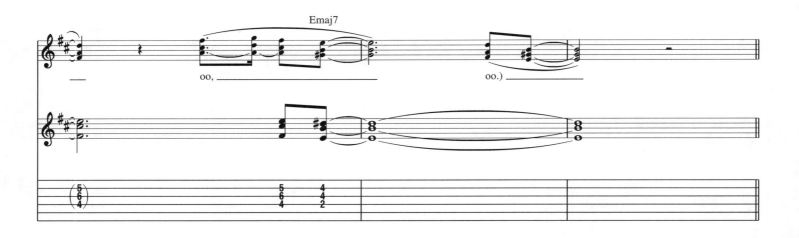

Emaj7

_   oo, _____   oo.) _____

Verse

Gtr. 2: w/ Rhy. Fig. 1 (4 times)
Gtr. 3: w/ Riff B (4 times)
Gtr. 5 tacet

Bm7   Bsus4

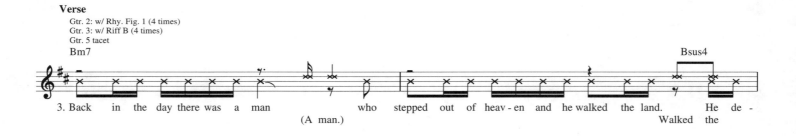

3. Back   in   the   day there was   a   man   who   stepped   out   of heav - en   and he walked   the land.   He de -
(A man.)   Walked   the

Bm7   Bsus4

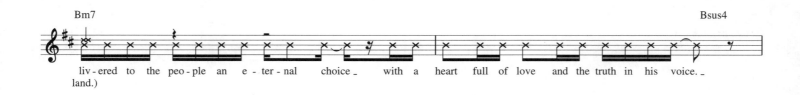

liv - ered   to   the   peo - ple   an   e - ter - nal   choice _   with   a   heart   full   of   love   and the truth   in   his   voice. _
land.)

Bm7   Bsus4

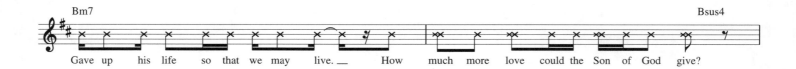

Gave   up   his   life   so   that   we   may   live. _   How   much   more   love   could   the   Son   of   God   give?

Bm7   Bsus4

Here is the ex - am - ple that we ought - ta be match - in' 'cause love is a word that re-quires some ac - tion.

⊕ Coda

Bkgd. Voc.: w/ Voc. Fig. 2 (3 3/4 times)
Gtrs. 3 & 4: w/ Rhy. Figs. 2 & 2A (1 7/8 times)
Gtr. 6: w/ Fill 1 (2 times)
E

Tell me, have - n't you heard. ____   Yeah. ____
(Hey, hey.   Love, love.)

Is a

Gtr. 6: w/ Fill 2
G

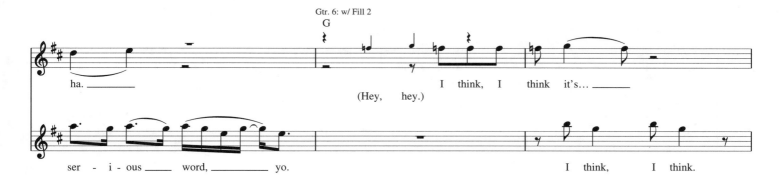

ha. ____   I think, I think it's… ____
(Hey,   hey.)

ser - i - ous ___ word, ____ yo.   I think,   I think.

1.
Gtr. 6: w/ Fill 1
B9   A   E

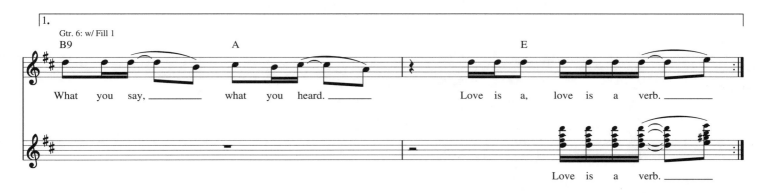

What you say, ____ what you heard. ____   Love is a, love is a verb. ____

Love is a verb. ____

2.
Gtr. 6: w/ Fill 1 (1st meas.)
B9   A   E   N.C.

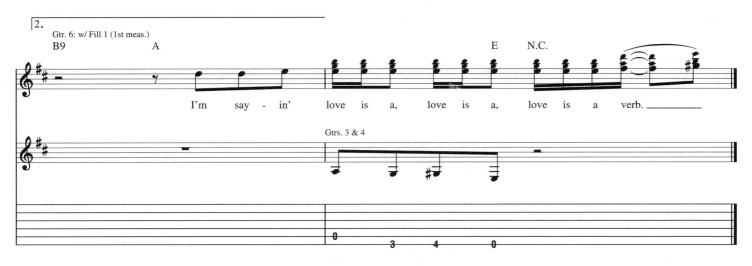

I'm say - in' love is a, love is a, love is a verb. ____

Gtrs. 3 & 4

Supernatural

Words and Music by Toby McKeehan, Michael Tait, Kevin Max and Mark Heimermann

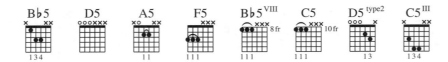

%. **Chorus**

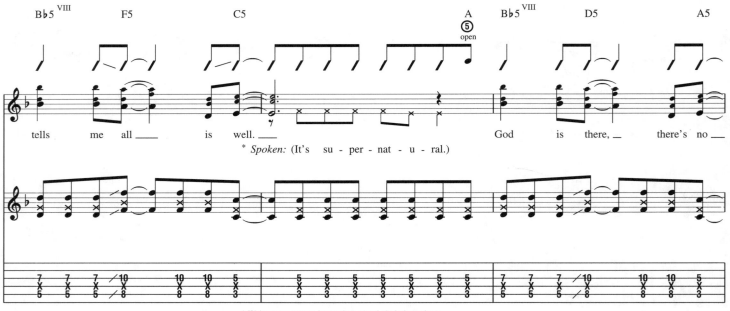

*Written one octave lower than actual pitch throughout.

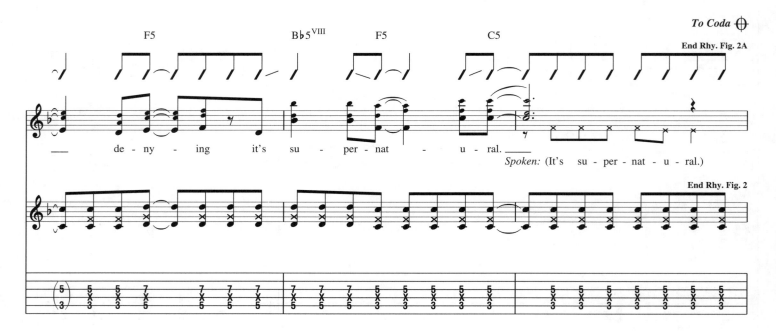

Bridge

Gtrs. 2 & 3: w/ Rhy. Fig. 1, simile

I need an in - ter - ven - tion. A touch of prov - i - dence.

D.S. al Coda

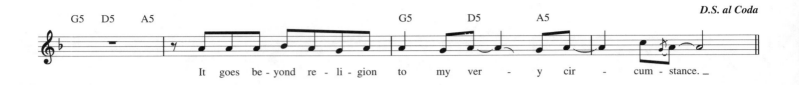

It goes be - yond re - li - gion to my ver - y cir - cum - stance.

⊕ *Coda*

Gtrs. 2 & 3: w/ Rhy. Figs. 2 & 2A, simile

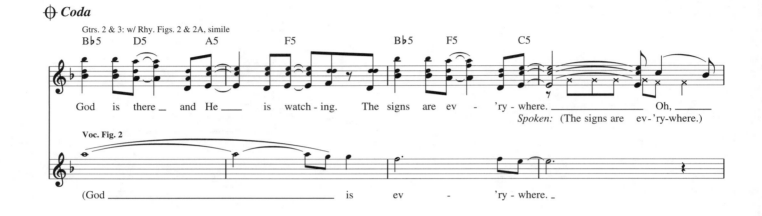

God is there and He is watch - ing. The signs are ev - 'ry - where. Oh,

Spoken: (The signs are ev - 'ry - where.)

Voc. Fig. 2

(God is ev - 'ry - where.

God is there. There's no de - ny - ing it's su - per - nat - u - ral.

Spoken: (It's su - per - nat - u - ral.)

End Voc. Fig. 2

God. Yeah.)

Interlude
Half-Time Feel

N.C.(Dm) (Bb/D) (Gm)

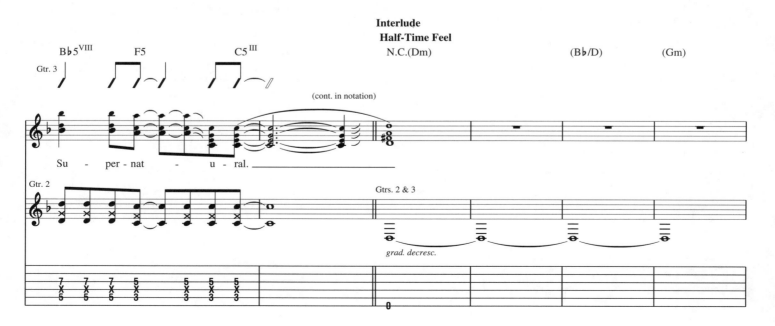

Gtr. 3

(cont. in notation)

Su - per - nat - u - ral.

Gtr. 2

Gtrs. 2 & 3

grad. decresc.

Gtrs. 2 & 3 tacet

(Dm)   (Bb)

Six days, a u - ni - verse ___ was made. ___

(Gm)   (Dm)   (Bb)

From the dead ___ a man ___ was raised. _____
(Raise. ___)

Voc. Fig. 3   End Voc. Fig. 3

(Su - per - nat - u - ral. ___)

Bkgd. Voc.: w/ Voc. Fig. 3   Bkgd. Voc.: w/ Voc. Fig. 3
(Gm)   (Dm)   (Bb)   (Gm)

They say He walked ___ a - cross ___ the waves. ___

(Dm)   (Bb)

And I'll be - lieve ___ it to my grave. _____

Bridge
N.C.(D5)
(tape effects)

Whispered: But I can see you com - ing.   You're not so far a - way.

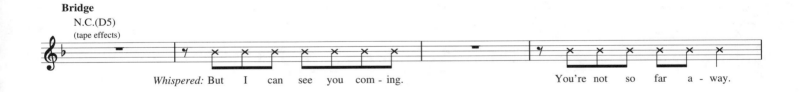

G5   D5   A5   G5   D5   A5

'Cause I can feel Your pow - er   Surg - ing through ___ the whole

Gtrs. 2 & 3

(cont. in slash)

Chorus

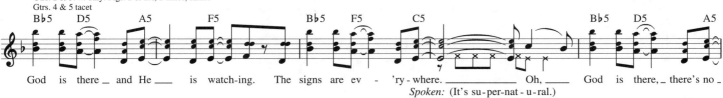

God is there __ and He __ is watch-ing. The signs are ev - 'ry-where. _____ Oh, __ God is there, there's no __

Spoken: (It's su-per-nat - u-ral.)

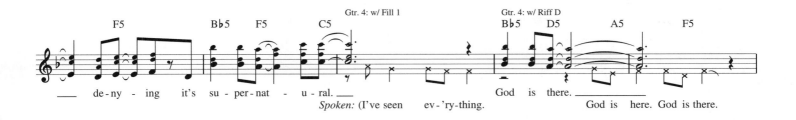

Gtr. 4: w/ Fill 1   Gtr. 4: w/ Riff D

__ de-ny - ing it's su-per-nat - u-ral. __ God is there. _____ God is here. God is there.

Spoken: (I've seen ev-'ry-thing.

Ev - 'ry-where. _____   Well, God is ev-'ry-where.   God is there. _____ God is here. God is there.

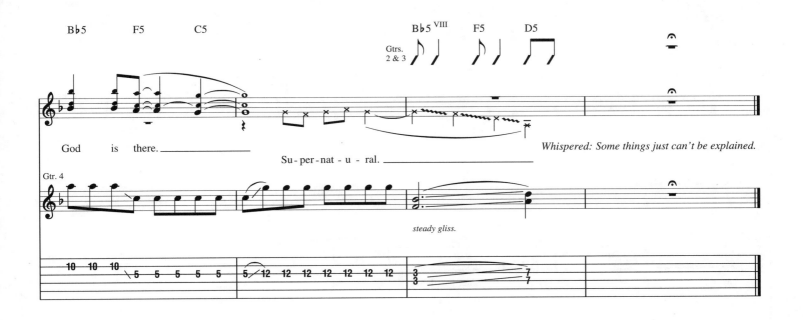

God is there. _____ _____   Su-per-nat - u - ral. _____   *Whispered: Some things just can't be explained.*

steady gliss.

Fill 1
Gtr. 3

103

Jesus Freak

Words and Music by Toby McKeehan and Mark Heimermann

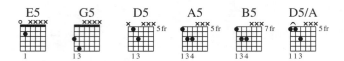

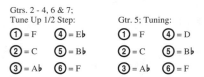

pronounced: Hey-soos

What will peo-ple think when they hear that I'm __ a Je - sus freak?
*(Je - sus __ freak - tus! __)

What will peo-ple do __ when they find out it's true? __

* Chord symbols and notation are respective to the combined tonality
  of the guitars in their altered tunings and do not reflect actual sounding chords.

* Chord symbols reflect overall tonality

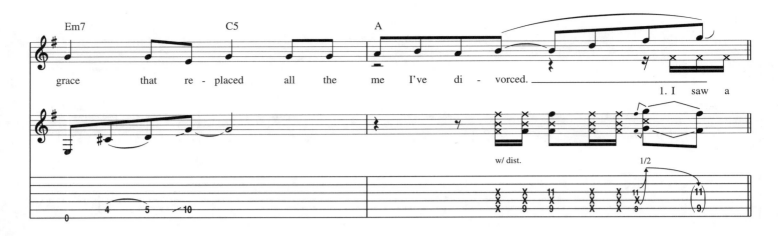

grace that re-placed all the me I've di-vorced. _____ 1. I saw a

Pre-Chorus

w/ Voc. Fill 1, 2nd time

man with a tat on his big fat bel-ly. It wrig-gled a-round like mar-ma-lade jel-ly. It
man from the des-ert with naps in his head. The sand that he walked was also his bed. The words

Gtr. 3 **Rhy. Fig. 2** **End Rhy. Fig. 2**

Gtr. 2

simile on repeat
let ring throughout

Gtr. 3: w/ Rhy. Fig. 2, 2 times

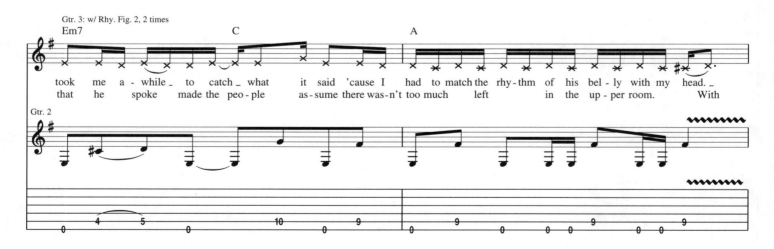

took me a-while _ to catch _ what it said 'cause I had to match the rhy-thm of his bel-ly with my head. _
that he spoke made the peo-ple as-sume there was-n't too much left in the up-per room. With

Gtr. 2

Voc. Fill 1

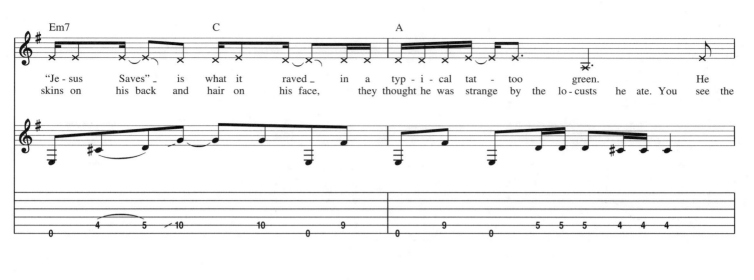

* Scrape edge of pick near bridge while holding the B note.

*Gtr. 2 tabbed to left of slash.

Bridge

People say I'm strange, does it ___ make me a stran-ger that my best friend ___ was born ___

___ in a man-ger? Peo-ple say I'm strange, ___ does it ___ make me a stran-ger that

my best friend ___ was born ___ in a man-ger? ___

Guitar Solo

The Hardway

Words and Music by Toby McKeehan

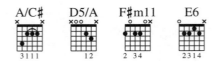

Tune down 1/2 step:
(low to high) Eb–Ab–Db–Gb–Bb–Eb

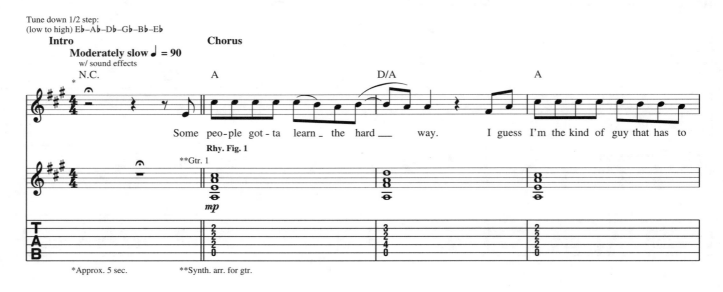

*Approx. 5 sec. **Synth. arr. for gtr.

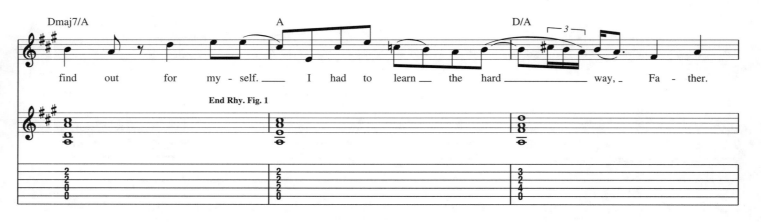

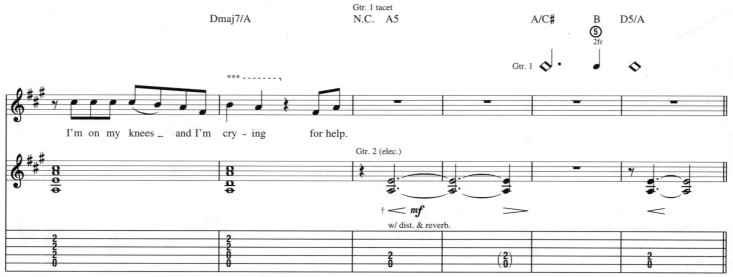

***w/ Echo set for half note regeneration w/ 3 repeats

†Vol. swell

I had to learn the hard way, Fa - ther. I'm on my knees and I'm cry - ing for your help,

*w/ Echo, set for half note regeneration
w/ 3 repeats.

Trumpet Solo

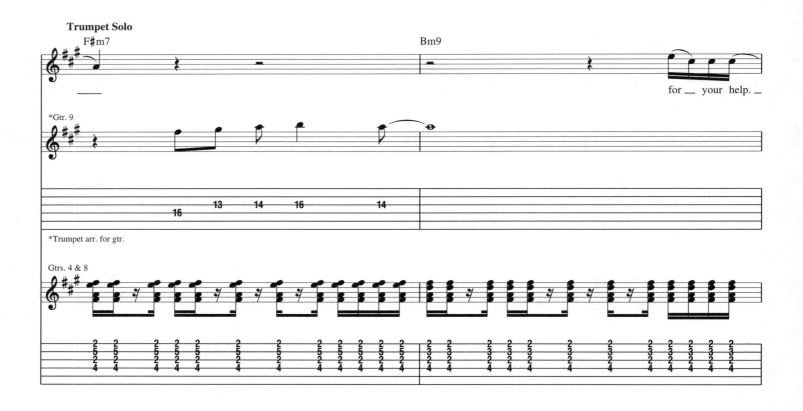

for your help.

*Gtr. 9

*Trumpet arr. for gtr.

Gtrs. 4 & 8

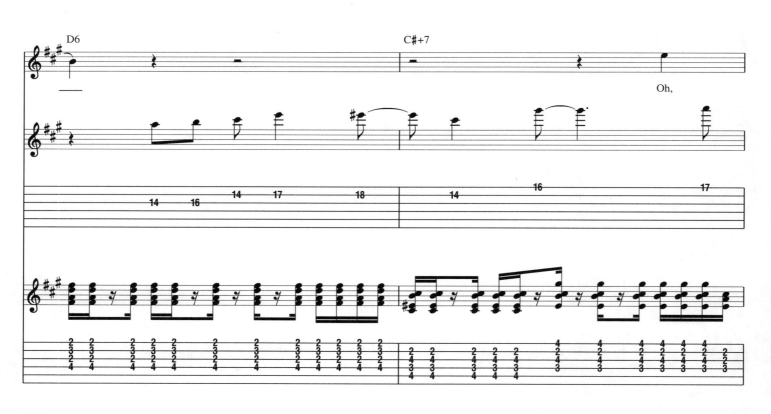

Oh,

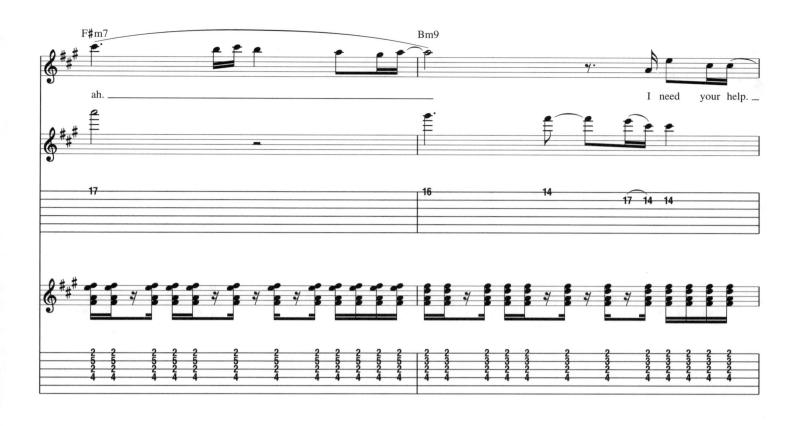

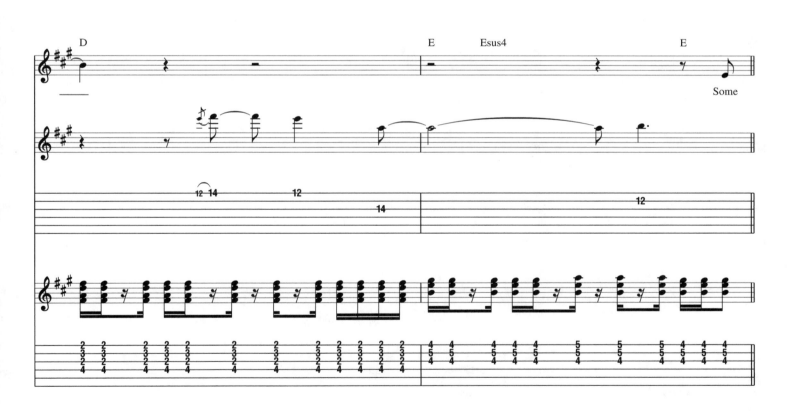

Chorus
Bkgd. Voc.: w/ Voc. Fig. 1 (2 times)
Gtr. 1: w/ Rhy. Fig. 1 (2 times)
Gtrs. 4, 8, & 9 tacet

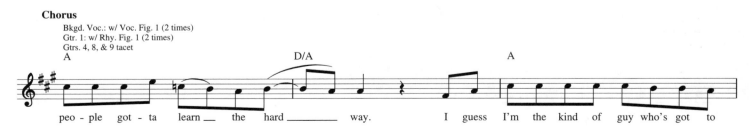

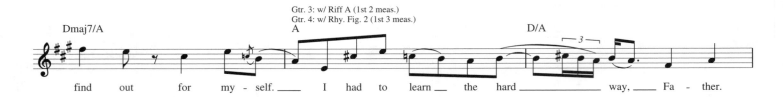

find out for my - self. ____ I had to learn ___ the hard _____ way, ___ Fa - ther.

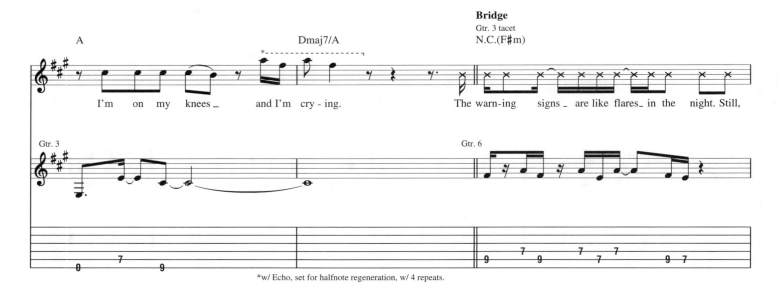

Bridge
Gtr. 3 tacet
N.C.(F#m)

I'm on my knees _ and I'm cry - ing. The warn-ing signs _ are like flares _ in the night. Still,

*w/ Echo, set for halfnote regeneration, w/ 4 repeats.

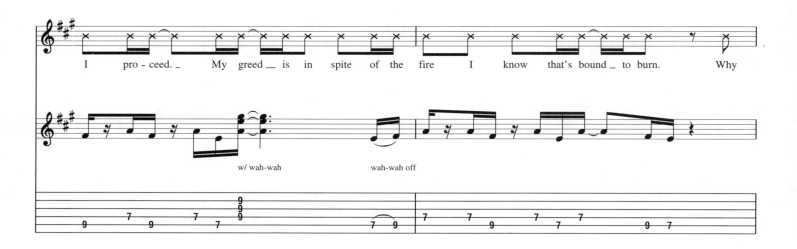

I pro - ceed. _ My greed _ is in spite of the fire I know that's bound _ to burn. Why

w/ wah-wah   wah-wah off

Outro
Bkgd. Voc.: w/ Voc. Fig. 1 (3 times)
Gtr. 1: w/ Rhy. Fig. 1 (3 times)
Gtr. 3: w/ Riff A (till end)
Gtr. 4: w/ Rhy. Fig. 2 (3 times)
Gtr. 6 tacet

is it that I al-ways got to learn the hard __ way, the hard __ way.

*w/ Echo, set for halfnote regeneration, w/ 1 repeat.   **As before

What If I Stumble

Words and Music by Toby McKeehan and Daniel Joseph

Spoken: The greatest single cause of atheism in the world today is Christians who acknowledge Jesus with their lips, and walk out the door and deny Him by their lifestyle. That is what an unbelieving world simply finds unbelievable.

* Key signature denotes D Dorian

** Chord symbols reflect implied tonality.

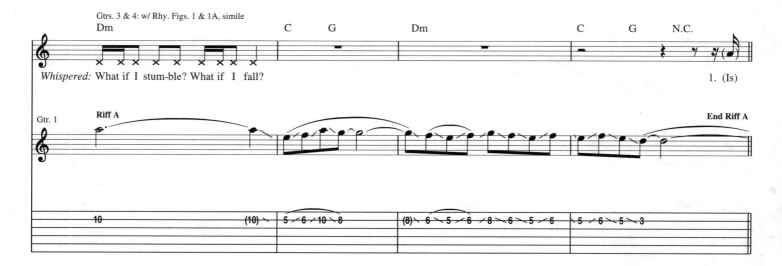

124

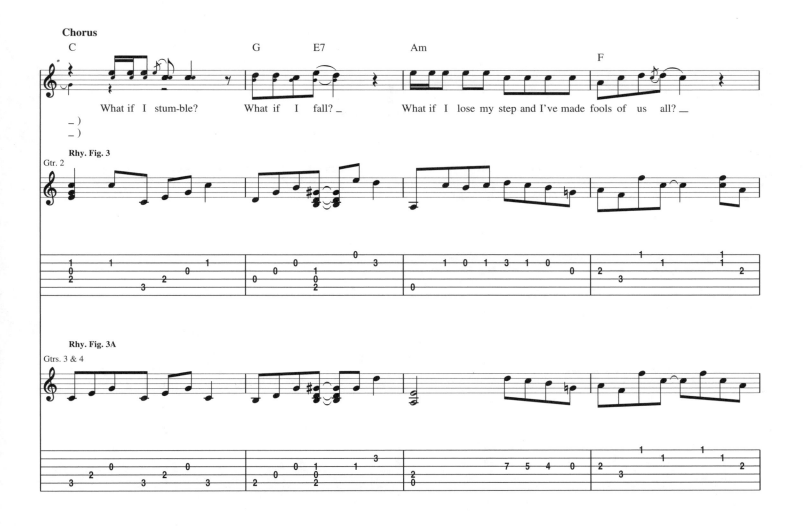

Interlude

Gtrs. 1, 2, 3 & 4: w/ Riff A & Rhy. Figs. 1 & 1A

fall? Whoa, _____ no. _____

(Ah. _____)

Whispered: What if I stum - ble? What if I fall? You nev - er turn in the heat of it all.

D.S. al Coda

What if I stun - ble? What is I fall? (echo repeats)

Coda

What if I stum - ble? _____ And what if I

Gtr. 2 **Rhy. Fig. 4** **End Rhy. Fig. 4**

Gtrs. 3 & 4 **Rhy. Fig. 4A** **End Rhy. Fig. 4A**

Mandolin Solo

Gtrs. 2, 3 & 4: w/ Rhy. Figs. 3 & 3A, simile

fall?

8va

* Gtr. 5

mf

* Mandolin arr. for gtr.

8va

I Wish We'd All Been Ready

Words and Music by Larry Norman

Chance

Words and Music by Toby McKeehan, Kevin Max, Michael Tait and Nathan December

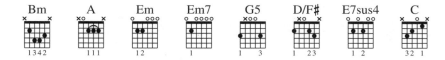

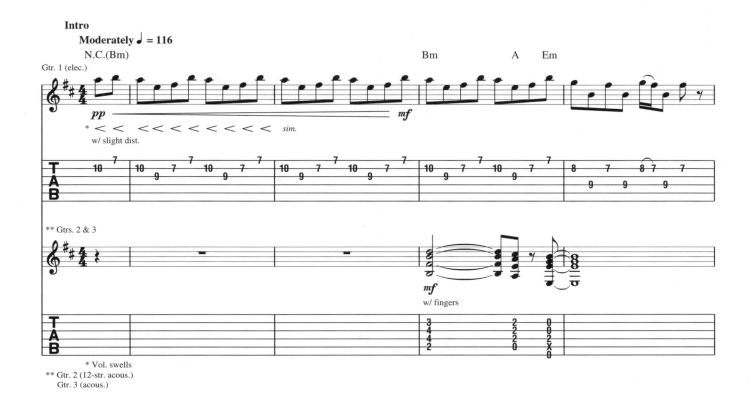

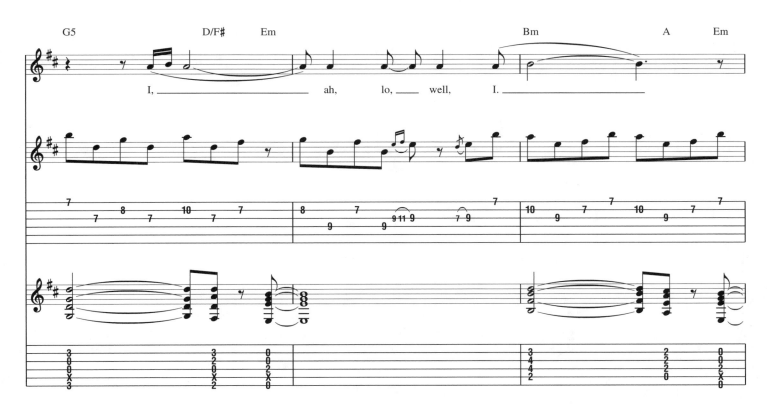

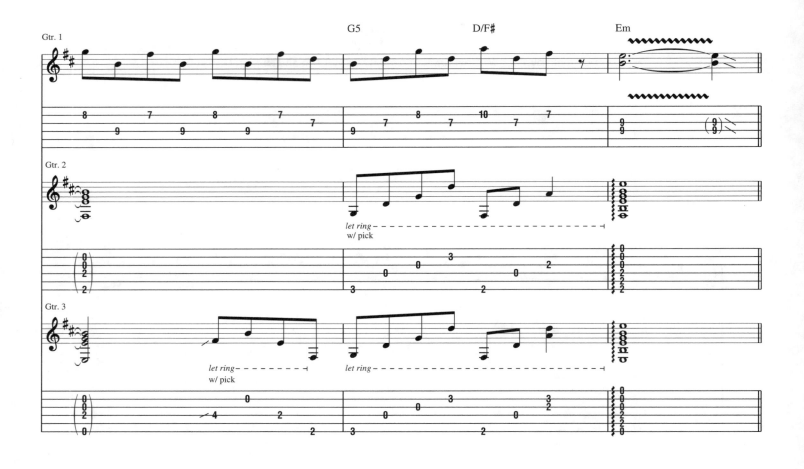

Verse

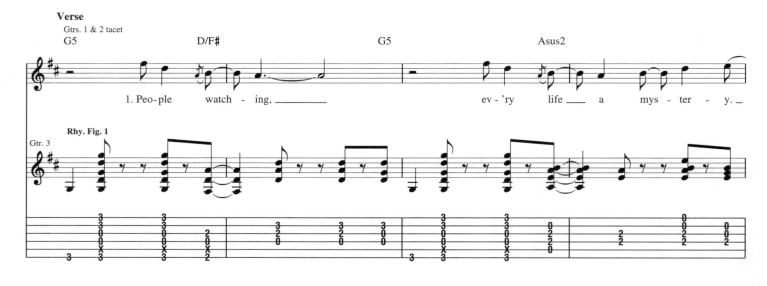

1. Peo-ple watch-ing, _____ ev-'ry life _ a mys-ter-y._

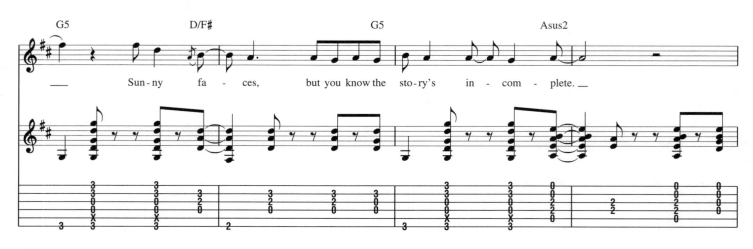

_ Sun-ny fa-ces, but you know the sto-ry's in-com-plete. _

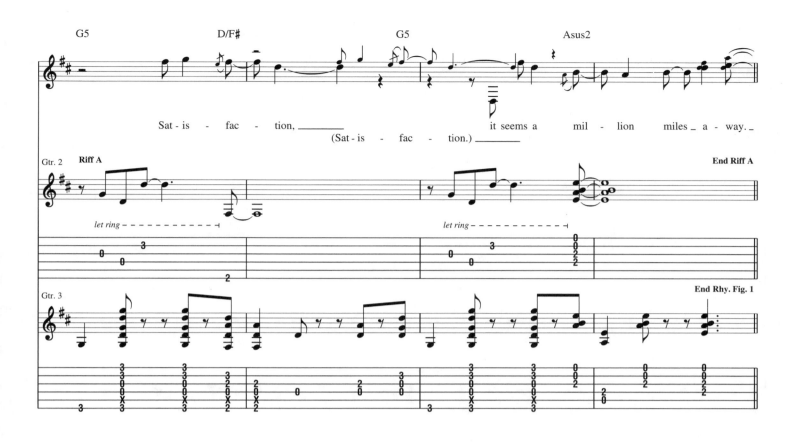

Sat - is - fac - tion, _____ it seems a mil - lion miles _ a - way. _

(Sat - is - fac - tion.) _____

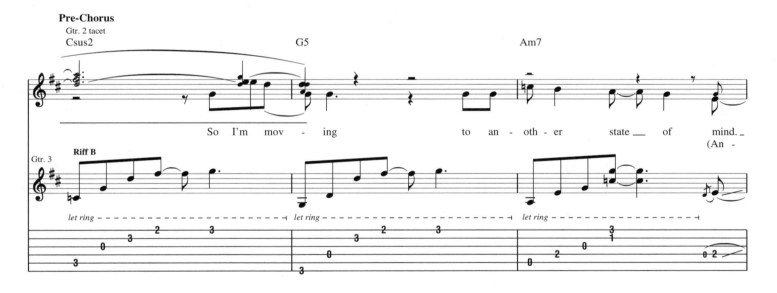

Pre-Chorus

So I'm mov - ing to an - oth - er state ___ of mind. _

(An -

oth - er state ___ of mind.) _____

I'm be - liev - ing there's no

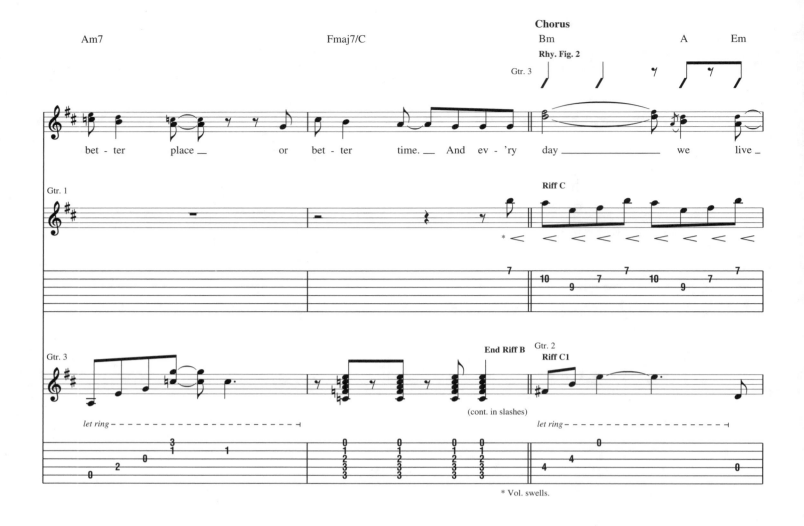

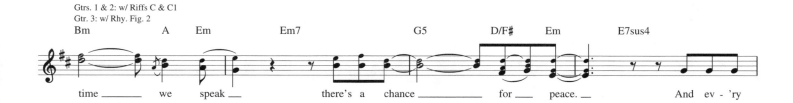

time _____ we speak ____ there's a chance _____ for ___ peace. ___ And ev - 'ry

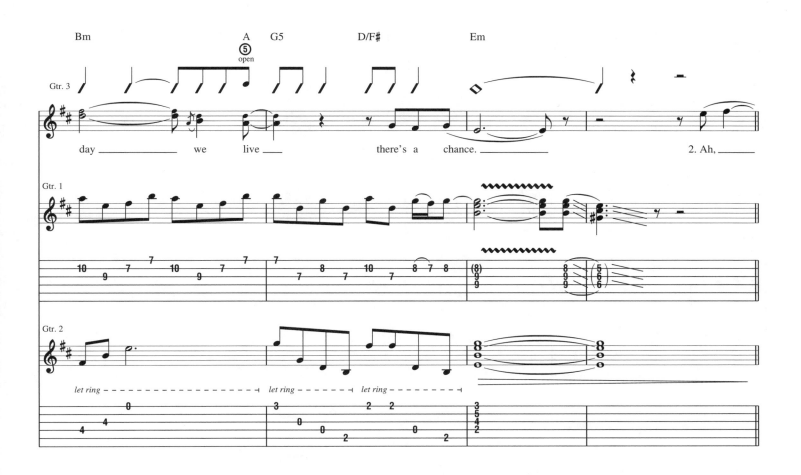

day _____ we live ____ there's a chance. _____ 2. Ah, _____

Verse

_____ lit - tle sis - ter, _____ put a - side ___ your fear ___ and breathe ___

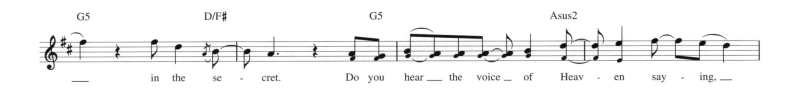

___ in the se - cret. Do you hear ___ the voice ___ of Heav - en say - ing, ___

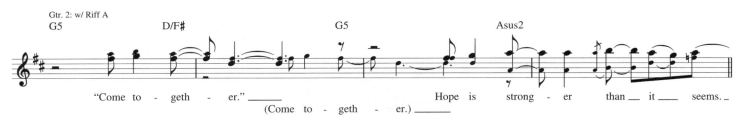

"Come to - geth - er." _____ Hope is strong - er than ___ it ___ seems. ___
(Come to - geth - er.) _____

Guitar Solo

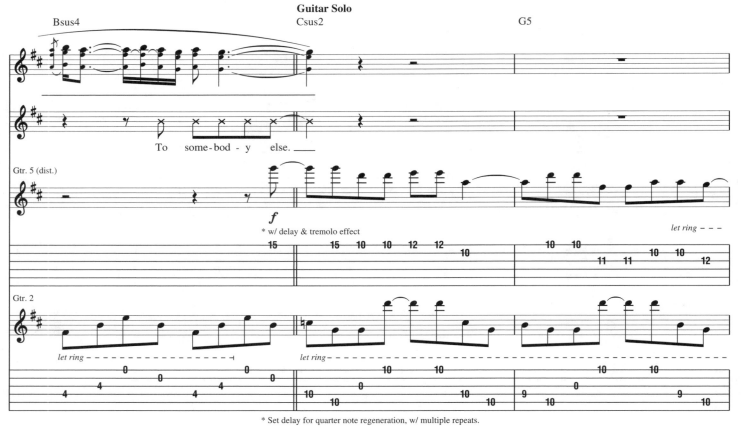

To some-bod-y else. ____

Gtr. 5 (dist.)

f

* w/ delay & tremolo effect

let ring - - -

Gtr. 2

let ring - - - - - - - - - - - - - -   *let ring - - - - - - - - -*

* Set delay for quarter note regeneration, w/ multiple repeats.

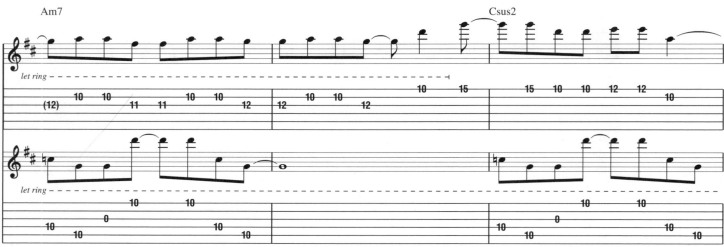

let ring -

let ring - - - - -

D.S. al Coda

And ev - 'ry

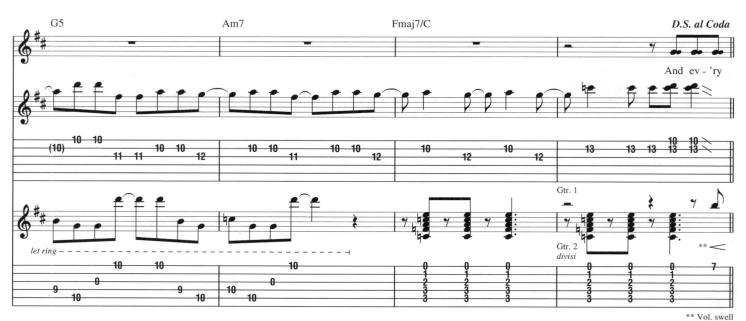

Gtr. 1

Gtr. 2
divisi

let ring - - - - - - - - - - - -

** Vol. swell

** Vol. swell

⊕ Coda

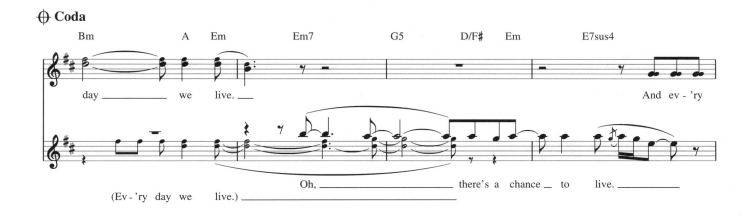

day _____ we live. _____
(Ev-'ry day we live.) _____

Oh, _____ there's a chance _ to live. _____

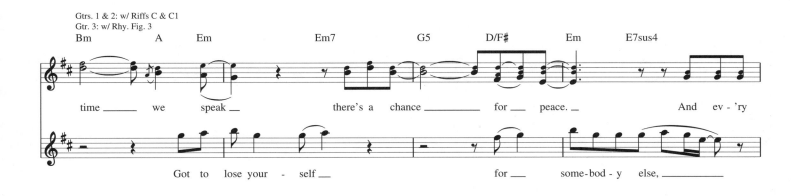

Gtrs. 1 & 2: w/ Riffs C & C1
Gtr. 3: w/ Rhy. Fig. 3

time _____ we speak _____ there's a chance _____ for _ peace. _ And ev-'ry

Got to lose your-self _____ for _ some-bod-y else, _____

day _____ we live. _ There's a chance. _
for some-bod-y, some-bod-y, yeah.

Oo, _ there's a chance. _
Ah. _____

Sugar Coat It

Words and Music by Toby McKeehan, Kevin Max and Mark Heimermann

Tune down 2 steps:
(low to high) C–F–B♭–E♭–G–C

Intro

Moderately ♩ = 120

N.C.(E7)

* Gtr. 1 (acous.)

Riff A / End Riff A

mf let ring / sim.

* Two gtrs. arr. for one.

Verse

Gtr. 1: w/ Riff A (3 times)

N.C.(E7)

1. Mov-ing at the speed of sound, __ there has nev-er been a lull in the mo - tion.

Con - ver - sa - tions swirl a - round, _____ stran - gers ques-tion-ing their de - vo - tion. _____

Wel-come to the world_ of talk __ shows __ where ev-'ry-bod-y seems to know. _____

Gtr. 2 (elec.)

mp

** w/ dist., phaser & octaver

** Set octaver for one octave below.

Pre-Chorus

Gtr. 2 tacet

*** B

D   A

Peo-ple talk __ and nev - er lis - ten. Come __ to their __ con-clu - sions _____ so we

Gtr. 4 (elec.)

Riff B1

mp

w/ dist.

Gtr. 3 (elec.)

Riff B

mp

w/ dist. & wah-wah

*** Chord symbols reflect overall harmony.

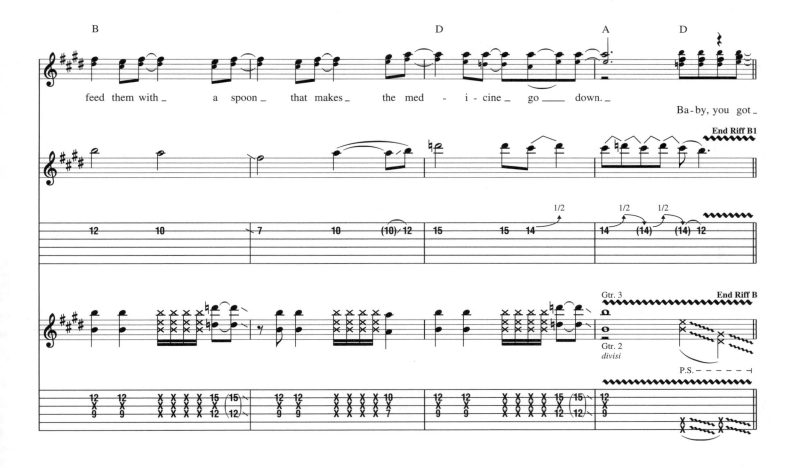

feed them with ___ a spoon ___ that makes ___ the med - i - cine ___ go ___ down. ___

Ba - by, you got ___

Chorus

Gtrs. 2, 3 & 4 tacet

___ it. Ba - by, we wrote ___ it. Ba - by, you thought ___ that we'd sug - ar coat ___

Gtr. 5 (elec.)

Riff C

mf

* w/ dist. & octaver

* Set octaver for one octave below.

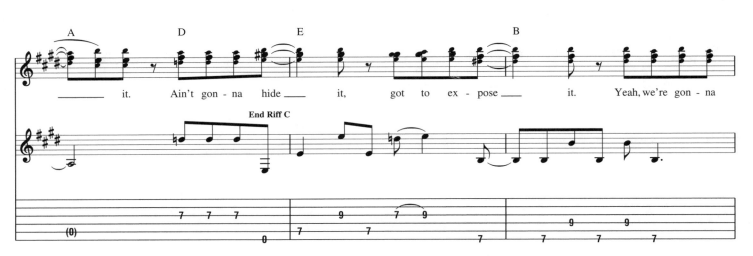

___ it. Ain't gon - na hide ___ it, got to ex - pose ___ it. Yeah, we're gon - na

End Riff C

let _____ our ____ light shine. _____

Gtr. 3

Gtr. 5

Verse
Gtr. 1: w/ Riff A (2 times)
Gtrs. 3 & 5 tacet

E7

2. Stand-ing in the stage of life ____ we are wait-ing for the fi - nal cur - tain. _____

You can take a seat and watch ___ to - night, ___ but you're gon-na get more than you came _

___ for. *Spoken:* Bam. And wel-come to our jam. And folks are get - ting down. The Je - sus freaks from

Gtr. 2

Let ____ our ____ light shine. _____ Let it shine. _

(Let it shine.) _____

Bridge
Gtr. 5 tacet
E7

Spoken: Boom. They thought we'd change our tune. They thought that we'd go

Gtr. 2
Riff D

bust. They thought we'd crum - ble like my grand - ma's fla - ky crust. Ka -

End Riff D

Gtr. 2: w/ Riff D

pow up in the here and now. The truth is scream - ing big, a light so bright wheth-er

N.C. **Interlude** N.C.(E)

day or night it can't be hid. Ba - by, ba - by, ba - by, you got _____ it.

* Fade in

(C) (E)

Ba - by, we wrote ____ it. Ain't gon - na hide ____ it.

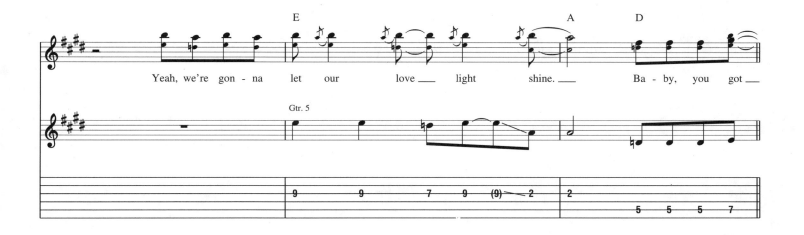

Yeah, we're gon - na let our love ___ light shine. ___ Ba - by, you got ___

Chorus

Gtr. 5: w/ Riff C (1 3/4 times)

___ it. Ba - by, we wrote ___ it. Ba - by, you thought ___ that we'd sug - ar coat ___

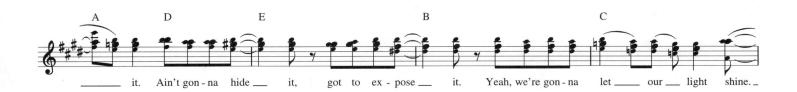

_____ it. Ain't gon - na hide ___ it, got to ex - pose ___ it. Yeah, we're gon - na let _____ our light shine. _

Outro-Chorus

Voc. Fig. 1

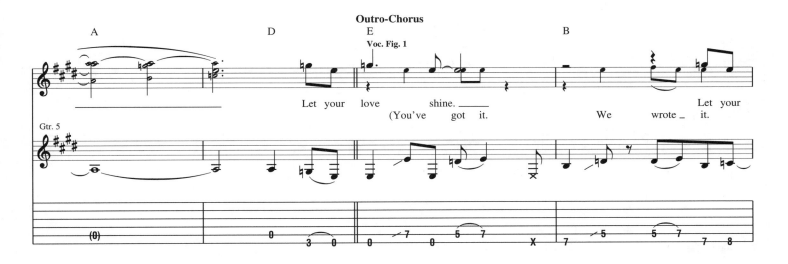

Let your love shine. _____
(You've got it. We wrote _ it. Let your

Gtr. 5

Bkgd. Voc.: w/ Voc. Fig. 1 (3 times)

End Voc. Fig. 1

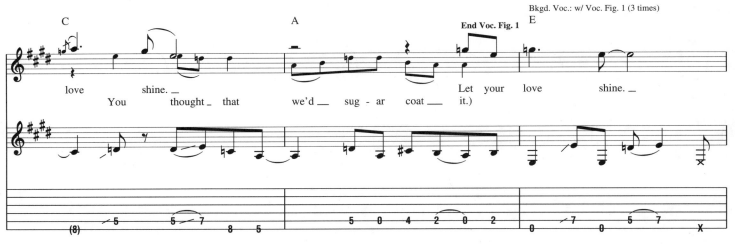

love shine. ___
You thought _ that we'd _ sug - ar coat ___ it.)
Let your love shine. _

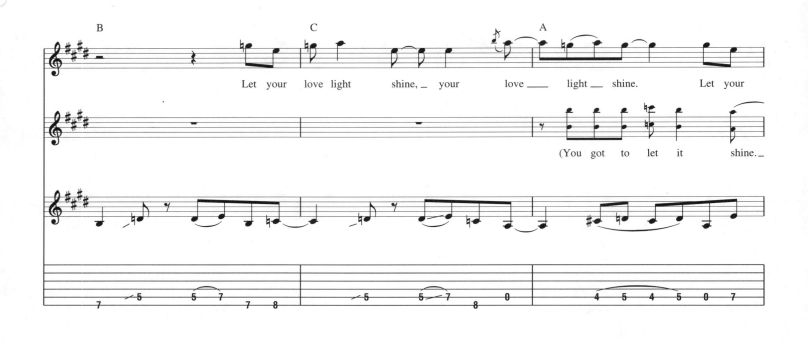

148

Guitar Notation Legend

Guitar Music can be notated three different ways: on a *musical staff*, in *tablature*, and in *rhythm slashes*.

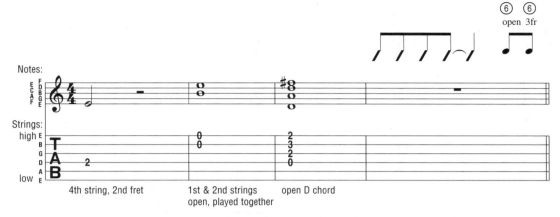

RHYTHM SLASHES are written above the staff. Strum chords in the rhythm indicated. Use the chord diagrams found at the top of the first page of the transcription for the appropriate chord voicings. Round noteheads indicate single notes.

THE MUSICAL STAFF shows pitches and rhythms and is divided by bar lines into measures. Pitches are named after the first seven letters of the alphabet.

TABLATURE graphically represents the guitar fingerboard. Each horizontal line represents a a string, and each number represents a fret.

4th string, 2nd fret   1st & 2nd strings open, played together   open D chord

Definitions for Special Guitar Notation

HALF-STEP BEND: Strike the note and bend up 1/2 step.

WHOLE-STEP BEND: Strike the note and bend up one step.

GRACE NOTE BEND: Strike the note and immediately bend up as indicated.

SLIGHT (MICROTONE) BEND: Strike the note and bend up 1/4 step.

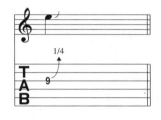

BEND AND RELEASE: Strike the note and bend up as indicated, then release back to the original note. Only the first note is struck.

PRE-BEND: Bend the note as indicated, then strike it.

PRE-BEND AND RELEASE: Bend the note as indicated. Strike it and release the bend back to the original note.

UNISON BEND: Strike the two notes simultaneously and bend the lower note up to the pitch of the higher.

VIBRATO: The string is vibrated by rapidly bending and releasing the note with the fretting hand.

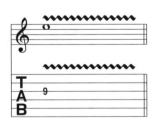

WIDE VIBRATO: The pitch is varied to a greater degree by vibrating with the fretting hand.

HAMMER-ON: Strike the first (lower) note with one finger, then sound the higher note (on the same string) with another finger by fretting it without picking.

PULL-OFF: Place both fingers on the notes to be sounded. Strike the first note and without picking, pull the finger off to sound the second (lower) note.

LEGATO SLIDE: Strike the first note and then slide the same fret-hand finger up or down to the second note. The second note is not struck.

SHIFT SLIDE: Same as legato slide, except the second note is struck.

TRILL: Very rapidly alternate between the notes indicated by continuously hammering on and pulling off.

TAPPING: Hammer ("tap") the fret indicated with the pick-hand index or middle finger and pull off to the note fretted by the fret hand.

NATURAL HARMONIC: Strike the note while the fret-hand lightly touches the string directly over the fret indicated.

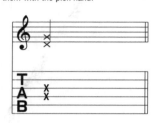

PINCH HARMONIC: The note is fretted normally and a harmonic is produced by adding the edge of the thumb or the tip of the index finger of the pick hand to the normal pick attack.

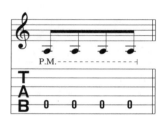

HARP HARMONIC: The note is fretted normally and a harmonic is produced by gently resting the pick hand's index finger directly above the indicated fret (in parentheses) while the pick hand's thumb or pick assists by plucking the appropriate string.

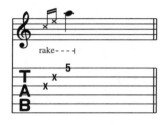

PICK SCRAPE: The edge of the pick is rubbed down (or up) the string, producing a scratchy sound.

MUFFLED STRINGS: A percussive sound is produced by laying the fret hand across the string(s) without depressing, and striking them with the pick hand.

PALM MUTING: The note is partially muted by the pick hand lightly touching the string(s) just before the bridge.

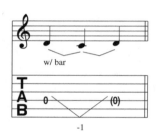

RAKE: Drag the pick across the strings indicated with a single motion.

TREMOLO PICKING: The note is picked as rapidly and continuously as possible.

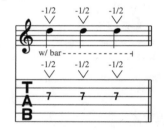

ARPEGGIATE: Play the notes of the chord indicated by quickly rolling them from bottom to top.

VIBRATO BAR DIVE AND RETURN: The pitch of the note or chord is dropped a specified number of steps (in rhythm) then returned to the original pitch.

VIBRATO BAR SCOOP: Depress the bar just before striking the note, then quickly release the bar.

VIBRATO BAR DIP: Strike the note and then immediately drop a specified number of steps, then release back to the original pitch.

Additional Musical Definitions

 (accent) • Accentuate note (play it louder)

(accent) • Accentuate note with great intensity

(staccato) • Play the note short

 • Downstroke

V • Upstroke

D.S. al Coda • Go back to the sign (𝄋), then play until the measure marked "*To Coda*," then skip to the section labelled "*Coda*."

D.C. al Fine • Go back to the beginning of the song and play until the measure marked "*Fine*" (end).

Rhy. Fig. • Label used to recall a recurring accompaniment pattern (usually chordal).

Riff • Label used to recall composed, melodic lines (usually single notes) which recur.

Fill • Label used to identify a brief melodic figure which is to be inserted into the arrangement.

Rhy. Fill • A chordal version of a Fill.

tacet • Instrument is silent (drops out).

 • Repeat measures between signs.

 • When a repeated section has different endings, play the first ending only the first time and the second ending only the second time.

NOTE: Tablature numbers in parentheses mean:
1. The note is being sustained over a system (note in standard notation is tied), or
2. The note is sustained, but a new articulation (such as a hammer-on, pull-off, slide or vibrato begins), or
3. The note is a barely audible "ghost" note (note in standard notation is also in parentheses).

christian**guitar**songbooks

BEST OF AUDIO ADRENALINE

This songbook features note-for-note transcriptions in standard notation & tab for 12 of their top hits: Big House • Can't Take God Away • Chevette • Get Down • Never Gonna Be as Big as Jesus • Walk on Water • more. Includes a band bio and photos.

_____00690418 Guitar Recorded Versions $17.95

BEST OF STEVEN CURTIS CHAPMAN

Features a dozen of his best songs, arranged for fingerstyle guitar: Busy Man • For the Sake of the Call • The Great Adventure • Heaven in the Real World • Hiding Place • His Eyes • His Strength Is Perfect • Hold On to Jesus • I Will Be Here • More to This Life • My Turn Now • What Would I Say.

_____00699138 Fingerstyle Guitar $10.95

BEST OF STEVEN CURTIS CHAPMAN FOR EASY GUITAR

15 songs including: The Great Adventure • Heaven in the Real World • His Strength Is Perfect • I Will Be There • More to This Life.

_____00702033 Easy Guitar with Notes & Tab $12.95

STEVEN CURTIS CHAPMAN GUITAR COLLECTION

12 of his most popular songs transcribed note-for-note for guitar, including: Fort the Sake of the Call • The Great Adventure • Heaven in the Real World • His Eyes • I Will Be Here • Lord of the Dance • More to This Life • Signs of Life • and more.

_____00690293 Guitar Recorded Versions $19.95

CONTEMPORARY CHRISTIAN FAVORITES

20 great easy guitar arrangements of contemporary Christian songs, including: El Shaddai • Friends • He Is Able • I Will Be Here • In the Name of the Lord • In Christ Alone • Love in Any Language • Open My Heart • Say the Name • Thy Word • Via Dolorosa • and more.

_____00702006 E-Z Guitar With Tab $10.95

CONTEMPORARY CHRISTIAN FAVORITES

17 great songs arranged for fingerstyle guitar: Butterfly Kisses • Chain of Grace • El Shaddai • Friend of a Wounded Heart • Friends • He Is Able • His Strength Is Perfect • Love in Any Language • Open My Heart • Say the Name • Thy Word • Via Dolorosa • more.

_____00699137 Fingerstyle Guitar $10.95

DC TALK – JESUS FREAK

Matching folio with note-for-note transcriptions to this contemporary Christian band's cross-over album. Songs include: Between You and Me • Jesus Freak • In the Light • Colored People • and more. Also includes photos.

_____00690184 Guitar Recorded Versions $19.95

DC TALK – SUPERNATURAL

Includes transcriptions in notes & tab of the 13 songs from Supernatural: Consume Me • Dive • Fearless • Godsend • Into Jesus • It's Killing Me • My Friend (So Long) • Red Letters • Since I Met You • Supernatural • There Is a Treason at Sea • The Truth • Wanna Be Loved.

_____00690333 Guitar Recorded Versions $19.95

DELIRIOUS? – MEZZAMORPHIS

14 songs in notes & tab from the third album by this Christian punk/pop band from England: Beautiful Sun • Blindfold • Bliss • Deeper 99 • Follow • Gravity • Heaven • It's OK • Jesus' Blood • Kiss Your Feet • Love Falls Down • Metamorphis • The Mezzanine Floor • See the Star. Includes photos.

_____00690378 Guitar Recorded Versions $19.95

FAVORITE HYMNS FOR EASY GUITAR

48 hymns, including: All Hail the Power of Jesus' Name • Amazing Grace • Be Thou My Vision • Blessed Assurance • Fairest Lord Jesus • I Love to Tell the Story • In the Garden • Let Us Break Bread Together • Rock of Ages • Were You There? • When I Survey the Wondrous Cross • and more.

_____00702041 E-Z Guitar with Notes & Tab $9.95

GLORIOUS HYMNS

Large, easy-to-read notation and tablature for 30 inspirational hymns: Abide with Me • Amazing Grace • Blessed Assurance • Come Christians Join to Sing • In the Garden • Jacob's Ladder • Rock of Ages • What a Friend We Have in Jesus • Wondrous Love • more.

_____00699192 EZ Play Guitar $7.95

GOSPEL FAVORITES FOR GUITAR

An amazing collection of 50 favorites, including: Amazing Grace • Did You Stop to Pray This Morning • He Lives • His Name Is Wonderful • How Great Thou Art • The King Is Coming • My God Is Real • Nearer, My God, To Thee • The Old Rugged Cross • Take My Hand, Precious Lord • Turn Your Radio On • Will the Circle Be Unbroken • and more.

_____00699374 EZ Guitar with Notes & Tab $14.95

BEST OF AMY GRANT

118 of her best arranged for easy guitar, including; Angels • Baby Baby • Big Yellow Taxi • Doubly Good to You • El Shaddai • Every Heartbeat • Find a Way • Good for Me • House of Love • Lead Me On • Lucky One • Tennessee Christmas • and more.

_____00702099 Easy Guitar with Notes & Tab......................$9.95

GREATEST HYMNS FOR GUITAR

48 hymns, including: Abide with Me • Amazing Grace • Be Still My Soul • Glory to His Name • In the Garden • and more.

_____00702116 Easy Guitar with Notes & Tab......................$7.95

MAKING SOME NOISE –TODAY'S MODERN CHRISTIAN ROCK

13 transcriptions, including: Big House • Cup • Flood • God • Jesus Freak • Shine • Soulbait • and more.

_____00690216 Guitar Recorded Versions $14.95

MXPX – THE EVER PASSING MOMENT

This matching folio to the release by this punk/pop Christian band includes note-for-note transcriptions for 15 tracks: Buildings Tumble • Educated Guess • Foolish • Here with Me • Is the Answer in the Question? • It's Undeniable • Misplaced Memories • My Life Story • The Next Big Thing • and more. Includes cool photos and tab.

_____00690448 Guitar Recorded Versions $19.95

THE BEST OF NEWSBOYS

13 songs in notes & TAB from these popular Christian rockers: Breakfast • Breathe • Dear Shame • Entertaining Angels • God Is Not a Secret • I Cannot Get You Out of My System • Real Good Thing • Shine • Spirit Thing • Step up to the Microphone • Strong Love • Take Me to Your Leader • Woo Hoo.

_____00690345 Guitar Recorded Versions $17.95

P.O.D. – THE FUNDAMENTAL ELEMENTS OF SOUTHTOWN

Matching folio with 16 songs, including: Bullet the Blue Sky • Follow Me • Freestyle • Image • Lie Down • Outkast • Rock the Party (Off the Hook) • Shouts • Southtown • and more.

_____00690456 Guitar Recorded Versions..........................$19.95

PRAISE AND WORSHIP FOR GUITAR

25 easy arrangements, including: As the Deer • Glorify Thy Name • He Is Exalted • Holy Ground • How Excellent Is Thy Name • Majesty • Thou Art Worthy • You Are My Hiding Place • more.

_____00702125 Easy Guitar with Notes & Tab $8.95

SONICFLOOD

6 songs transcribed note-for-note, including: Carried Away • Holy One • I Could Sing of Your Love Forever • I Need You • My Refuge • There's Something About That Name.

_____00690385 Guitar Recorded Versions $19.95

TODAY'S CHRISTIAN FAVORITES

19 songs, including: Daystar • Find Us Faithful • Go West Young Man • God and God Alone • He Is Exalted • I Will Choose Christ • Jubilate • My Turn Now • A Perfect Heart • Revive Us, O Lord • and more.

_____00702042 Easy Guitar with Notes & Tab $8.95

TODAY'S CHRISTIAN ROCK FOR EASY GUITAR

Over 10 powerful contemporary Christian songs. Includes: Between You and Me (dc Talk) • Flood (Jars of Clay) • Kiss Me (Sixpence None the Richer) • Lord of the Dance (Steven Curtis Chapman) • On My Knees (Jaci Velasquez) • and more.

_____00702124 Easy Guitar with Notes & Tab $8.95

Prices and availability subject to change without notice.

FOR MORE INFORMATION, SEE YOUR LOCAL MUSIC DEALER, OR WRITE TO:

HAL•LEONARD®
CORPORATION
7777 W. BLUEMOUND RD. P.O. BOX 13819 MILWAUKEE, WI 53213

www.halleonard.com

ALL BOOKS INCLUDE NOTES & TABLATURE